TRADITIONS

A GUIDEBOOK

FROM THE MUSEUM OF SCIENCE AND INDUSTRY'S
"CHRISTMAS AROUND THE WORLD" AND "HOLIDAYS OF LIGHT" FESTIVALS.

The Museum of Science and Industry, Chicago
Copyright© 1999 The Museum of Science and Industry, Chicago
57th Street and Lake Shore Drive
Chicago, Illinois 60637
1-773-684-1414

Library of Congress Catalog Number: 99-074680
ISBN: 0-9638657-7-3

For The Museum of Science and Industry, Chicago:
President and CEO: David R. Mosena
Vice President of Guest Services: Nancy L. Wright
Manager of Product Development: Jennifer J. Wood
Writer: Erin Okamoto Protsman

Photography by: Joe Ziolkowski
Assisted by: Matthew Wagner

Designed, edited, and manufactured by
Favorite Recipes® Press
an imprint of

FRP

P.O. Box 305142
Nashville, TN 37230
1-800-358-0560

Art Director: Steve Newman
Project Manager: Elizabeth Miller, JD
Book Designer: Bill Kersey

Manufactured in the United States of America
First Printing: 1999   8,000 copies

DEDICATION

The Museum of Science and Industry developed TRADITIONS
as a lasting tribute to all of the community organizations,
past and present, that have participated in "Christmas Around
the World" and "Holidays of Light" over the years.
These organizations' support for the Museum and their
rich cultural heritage show in the trees that they decorate,
the expressive songs they sing, the detailed displays they create,
and the stories they tell.

PREFACE

There is so much to see and enjoy during the holidays, not just near our homes, but around the globe. Through the years, the Museum of Science and Industry has developed a close working relationship with the Chicago area ethnic communities. While working on the "Christmas Around the World" and "Holidays of Light" exhibits, many representatives have generously shared with us their holiday-related experiences, customs, traditions, and folk tales of celebrations in lands near and far. Through additional research we have uncovered even more entertaining facts and holiday folklore. We would like to share these stories with our readers.

This book is meant to give our readers a glimpse of holidays past and present. It is by no means a representation of all winter holidays, nor is it meant to suggest that all people from one country celebrate the holidays in the exact same way. Traditions vary from region to region and family to family. The following information represents just a small sample of the richness of cultures and the diversified beauty that is "Christmas Around the World" and "Holidays of Light."

FOREWORD

Dear Friends,

The Museum of Science and Industry's "Christmas Around the World" tradition began in the early 1940s as a United Nations Day salute to American allies during the war. The original event brought together our friends and neighbors, sharing the different ways Christmas was celebrated across the globe. Since then, millions of visitors have enjoyed this annual exhibition. For some, "seeing the trees" has become a treasured family tradition.

Each November, groups from Chicago's diverse ethnic communities come together to decorate an enchanting forest of trees. Featuring hand-made crafts and ornaments passed from one generation to the next, each tree glitters uniquely, created with careful hands and cultural pride.

In 1994, the "Christmas Around the World" program was expanded to celebrate multi-cultural observances of light and enlightenment. "Holidays of Light" includes celebrations such as Chinese New Year, Hanukkah, and Saint Lucia Day.

The Museum's annual program offers visitors a rare opportunity to peek into a "global living room" and to share in holiday festivities from Poland to Puerto Rico, from Iceland to India.

Most importantly, the "Christmas Around the World" and "Holidays of Light" festivals brings people together—it honors the stories and traditions that make us unique and celebrates the values that we all share.

Our international family—the dedicated people who create our "Christmas Around the World" and "Holidays of Light" displays each year—have gone one step further to bring the holidays home. They've contributed stories and holiday traditions from their homelands to share with you and your family during the holiday season.

We hope you'll enjoy this very special treasure of memories.

DAVID R. MOSENA

President and CEO

INTRODUCTION

Experiencing the magic of the Museum of Science and Industry's "Christmas Around the World" festival has become an annual holiday tradition for hundreds of thousands of Chicago area families and friends. Who would have guessed that this simple celebration would grow to be such a popular Chicago custom, standing the test of time for well over five decades?

The Museum's first Christmas festival was created in 1942 by the late Major Lenox Lohr, the Museum's first president. The festival was Lohr's way of honoring Chicago's ethnic communities whose native countries were allied with the United States during World War II. During the festival's first year, one live Christmas tree was featured. With the help of volunteers recruited from various Chicago communities, this lone tree was decorated each evening by a different group for display the following morning. The Christmas tree stood in the Museum for only two weeks and featured handmade ornaments from around the world. Traditional ethnic holiday foods were served at lunch time, and flags from twenty-nine nations were suspended from the balcony in the Museum's North Court.

This first effort was so popular that the Museum invited the ethnic communities back the following year. This time, each group decorated its own individual tree to resemble trees from its cultural heritage. Theater pageants also were added to the festivities, treating visitors to songs, dances, and celebrations of different cultures. Although the display was named first "Christmas in the United Nations" and later "Around the World at Christmas," the celebration was dubbed "Christmas Around the World" in the late 1940s. As the decades passed, "Christmas Around the World" became increasingly popular with visitors, and the Museum enjoyed the support of more and more community organizations that wanted to share their holiday customs.

In 1994, the Museum's holiday festivities expanded further to include a new display called "Holidays of Light." This multicultural exhibit celebrates a variety of holidays that feature light or enlightenment as the central theme. Each year, eight holidays are highlighted in displays encased in a stunning flame sculpture. It is open during the same time as "Christmas Around the World" to show visitors the diversity of winter festivals from around the globe.

Today, the "Christmas Around the World" and "Holidays of Light" festivals are supported by over sixty ethnic communities and organizations throughout the Chicago area. Visitors enjoy the sights and sounds of the holidays as they walk through a forest of more than forty beautifully decorated Christmas trees and creches, and they marvel at the displays in the equally striking "Holidays of Light" sculpture. Visitors also are treated to an extensive array of international pageants and programming designed to satisfy many different tastes.

Before visitors see "Christmas Around the World" and "Holidays of Light" in their completed states, thousands of people from the community spend hours, days, weeks, and months researching displays, perfecting dance steps, and decorating the Christmas trees. It is during this preparation time, when the representatives and their families are at the Museum, that people reminisce about beloved traditions, tell favorite folk tales, and reveal forgotten holiday customs. The Museum of Science and Industry has committed many of these stories to paper in *Traditions*. These are the holiday stories and traditions that help define cultures and keep families, friends, and neighbors young at heart.

Traditions is a lasting tribute to all the community groups and organizations, past and present, who have participated in "Christmas Around the World" and "Holidays of Light" over the years. Their support of the Museum and their love of their cultures show in the intricate ornaments they make, the expressive songs they sing, the detailed displays they create, and the rich stories they tell. The Museum wishes to express its grateful appreciation to all the individuals and organizations who have contributed generously to the making of this book.

Erin Okamoto Protsman

*Indicates Christmas
Around the World*

*Indicates Holidays
of Light*

CONTENTS

CHRISTMAS AROUND THE WORLD

CZECH REPUBLIC 32

DENMARK 34

ECUADOR 36

EGYPT 38

FINLAND 40

FRANCE 42

GERMANY 44

GREECE 46

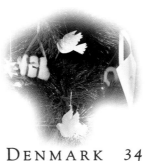

GUATEMALA 48

CHRISTMAS AROUND THE WORLD

CHRISTMAS AROUND THE WORLD

CHRISTMAS AROUND THE WORLD

SCOTLAND 86

SERBIA 88

SLOVENIA 90

SWEDEN 92

SWITZERLAND 94

UKRAINE 96

WALES 98

HOLIDAY OF LIGHTS

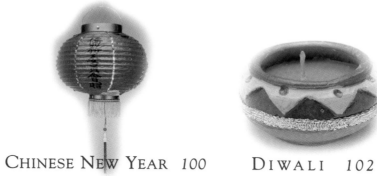

ARMENIA

SOORP GANOOK

WHITE DOVES COVER THE TREE; THESE PEACE-SEEKING BIRDS SERVE AS A REMINDER OF NOAH'S ARK, WHICH LANDED ON ARMENIA'S MOUNT ARARAT. BLUE LIGHTS AND THE STAR OF BETHLEHEM ON TOP RECOUNT THE PEACE AND CALM OF THE NIGHT JESUS WAS BORN SO MANY YEARS AGO.

It seems only fitting for Armenia, the first nation to adopt Christianity, to celebrate both Christmas and Jesus' baptism on the same day. On January 6, people gather at church for the *Churorhnek* (the Blessing of the Water) which commemorates the day John the Baptist baptized Jesus in the River Jordan. During this ceremony, a basin of water is blessed, and holy oil is poured into the basin to signify the appearance of the Holy Spirit. Upon the ceremony's end, people fill containers with the water to take home. This water then is mixed with earth and used symbolically to clean household items. The rest of Christmas Day is spent visiting with friends and relatives.

Prior to Christmas Day, Armenians prepare their homes for the upcoming holidays. Often priests visit during the season, blessing the home with salt and water. Those who long for winter to end pour lentils, chickpeas, or wheat seeds into a pot of water-saturated cotton balls. In less than a week, tiny sprouts appear, bringing new life into the home. The potted sprouts rapidly grow, making a green and lush centerpiece.

To teach children the importance of Christmas, most families display nativity scenes. Ranging from simple to elaborate, the figurines help tell the story of Christ's birth. In addition to the nativity scenes, decorating Christmas trees also is becoming increasingly popular. White doves cover the tree; these peace-seeking birds serve as a reminder of Noah's Ark, which landed on Armenia's Mount Ararat. Blue lights and the Star of Bethlehem on top recount the peace and calm of the night Jesus was born so many years ago.

One week prior to Christmas, Armenians fast, eliminating animal products from their diet. The fast ends on Christmas Eve immediately following church services. In honor of Mary, it is customary to eat fried fish, lettuce, and spinach, believed to be the same meal she ate on the eve of her Son's birth. Other popular dishes include roasted lamb, vegetables, buttery braided bread, rice pilaf, rice pudding, figs, baklava, and a dish of *anoushabour* (Christmas pudding made from whole wheat berries and apricots).

Throughout the holiday season, there are many traditions enjoyed especially by the young. Children have great fun hanging their handkerchiefs from the roofs' edge. Climbing to the rooftops, children sing, "Rejoice and be glad! Open your bag, and fill our handkerchiefs! Hallelujah! Hallelujah!" Much to the children's delight, adults good-naturedly climb to the handkerchiefs, filling them with money, fried wheat, and raisins. Opportunities for gifts are not limited to the rooftops. On New Year's Eve, children anxiously wait for a visit from their beloved *Gah-ghant Baba* (Old Father), a kind gentleman similar to Santa Claus. Each year, *Gah-ghant Baba* delivers presents to all good boys and girls, making the New Year a special time in the hearts of children.

AUSTRIA

FROEHLICHE WEINACHTEN

ON CHRISTMAS EVE NIGHT, ONCE CHILDREN HEAR THE
TINKLING OF BELLS, A MAGNIFICENT FIR TREE GLOWING WITH
CANDLELIGHT APPEARS FROM BEHIND CLOSED DOORS. CAREFULLY
STACKED PRESENTS LIE UNDERNEATH THE TREE.

The holiday season begins when *Heiliger Nikolaus* (Saint Nicholas) and his sidekick Krampus arrive in town and children clamor to tell them all the good or bad things they have done since their last visit. Krampus, a grotesque-looking devil, tries to whip the children who admit to naughtiness. However, *Heiliger Nikolaus* rewards the boys and girls with nuts, apples, and sweets if they promise to be good. On Saint Nicholas Day Eve, December 5, children leave their boots by the front door, hoping *Heiliger Nikolaus* will fill them with gifts.

Hanging the Advent wreath on the front door is another sign that Christmas is coming. Holiday decorations include a nativity scene prominently displayed in the home. In many families, the figurines are hand carved in intricate detail and passed down from generation to generation. Parents decorate the Christmas tree in secret so that the children will not see it before Christmas Eve. In rural areas, straw ornaments are popular, while in cities, handblown glass ornaments adorn the tree. Tissue-wrapped candles, flowers, ribbon, and cookies fill the remaining branches. An angel takes her place of honor on top of the tree, completing the breathtaking vision.

During the holiday season, people are busy cooking and baking delicious things to eat. *Stollen* (a holiday bread), Saint Nicholas-shaped ginger cookies, and *Spanischer Wind* (meringue and nut cookies) are gobbled up. The cookies often are strung with ribbon and hung on the tree. Carp is a holiday must, which is served along with family favorites such as roast goose, sweet cheese, and gingerbread topped with beer sauce. Viennese coffee accompanies these holiday treats.

On Christmas Eve night, once children hear the tinkling of bells, a magnificent fir tree glowing with candlelight appears from behind closed doors. Carefully stacked presents lie underneath the tree. Children look in awe, knowing that the Christ Child has left the beautiful tree and the gifts especially for them. After Christmas Eve, everyone is allowed to eat the treats off the tree. Until it is time to leave for Midnight Mass, the family admires the tree and joyously sings Christmas carols.

One of the most beloved Christmas carols, "Silent Night," was written one Christmas shortly before a Midnight Mass. In Oberndorf, back in 1818, Father Joseph Mohr discovered to his horror that mice had eaten through the bellows of the church organ. Badly damaged, the organ could not be played for the Christmas Eve church service. Father Mohr and the church organist, Franz Gruber, frantically tried to write a song in place of organ music. Uninspired, Gruber peered out of his window and was moved by the silent and holy night. Suddenly, he had an idea for a song! Father Mohr completed the verses when he saw beams of moonlight streaming through the stained glass, illuminating a mother comforting her newborn child. The words "Round yon virgin mother and child" came to him, and together Mohr and Gruber finished the song. That evening during Midnight Mass, Gruber played his guitar while Father Mohr sang the song.

BELGIUM

JOYEUX NOËL

VROLIJK KERSTFEEST

BELGIAN FAMILIES RELY ON SIMPLE CHRISTMAS
DECORATIONS. THEY ENHANCE THE BEAUTY OF THE PINE
TREE WITH WHITE CANDLES OR ELECTRIC LIGHTS.

In this small northwestern European country, the holiday season begins on December 6, Saint Nicholas Day, and ends on January 6 with the Epiphany. Before World War II, Belgians celebrated Christmas quietly and reverently. The events that highlighted the holiday season were Christmas Eve church services followed by a family feast.

Sint Niklaas (Saint Nicholas) is popular among children and the young at heart. The legend is based on the life of the Bishop of the church of Myra in Lycia. Around 350 A.D. when it was not popular to treat children with kindness and patience, the Bishop preached to the people the importance of acting compassionately towards children. He is best remembered for saving three impoverished girls who wanted to marry but could not because they did not have dowries. For each girl, the kind Bishop threw a bag of gold through their windows at night so that their wishes of an honorable marriage could come true. Because he showered children in love and kindness, he became the patron saint of children, known as Saint Nicholas. To this day, people give each other gifts in honor of his generosity.

On Saint Nicholas Day Eve, children welcome the good Bishop as he ambles down the streets on his donkey. Later that evening, children place their slippers in front of their bedroom doors. In the night he fills the slippers with candy and small gifts.

In the past fifty years, Belgian Christmas customs changed and expanded to include other European traditions, such as the German custom of decorating the Christmas tree. A few days before Christmas Eve, a member of the family selects a pine tree and brings it in the home for decoration. Belgian families rely on simple Christmas decorations. They enhance the beauty of the pine tree with white candles or electric lights. Some families also drape white angel hair, cottony threads as delicate as a spider's web, on the tree. A star representing the Star of Bethlehem or an angel tops the tree. Belgians also display a *crèche* (nativity scene) in their homes. No other decorations are needed. The *crèche* and tree are sufficient to celebrate the true meaning of Christmas.

As in the past, Christmas Eve supper is served immediately following Midnight Mass. Once the meal is over, the youngest member of the family places the Baby Jesus gently down in the *crèche's* manger of hay. Christmas Day is spent quietly, highlighted by a large feast featuring the family's favorite dishes. Of course, tasty *speculoos* (spiced ginger cookies shaped as *Sint Niklaas*) are baked continuously and on hand throughout the holiday season.

The long holiday season ends on the Epiphany. On this day, the Three Wise Men figurines are placed in the *crèche*, which symbolizes their arrival in Bethlehem. With the arrival of the Three Wise Men, the *crèche*, at last, is complete.

To commemorate the Epiphany, a moist cake is served for dessert. Hidden inside the cake is a bean. The person who finds the bean is crowned king or queen for the day, in honor of the Magi present at Christ's birth.

BELIZE

BUITI SEDU

FELIZ NAVIDAD

WELL AFTER MIDNIGHT, WHEN THE FAMILY RETURNS
FROM MASS, CHILDREN ARE ALLOWED TO OPEN THEIR
PRESENTS BEFORE GOING TO BED.

Communities unite for good-natured fun during this festive holiday season. Although Belize is the only English-speaking country in Central America, its diversified population adds to the richness of a three-day celebration, which begins on Christmas Eve, December 24, and ends with Boxing Day, December 26.

Holiday activities begin on Christmas Eve night with Midnight Mass. While the family worships in church, Santa Claus flies through the sky from his home at the North Pole. He leaves gifts under the family's pine tree, which is decorated with wooden boat ornaments and bird ornaments carved from coconut shells. Well after midnight, when the family returns from Mass, children are allowed to open their presents before going to bed.

As late as one or two in the morning, "Boom and Chime" bands travel from house to house, serenading neighbors with calypso music. The musicians, playing instruments made from coconut graters, pots, and spoons, make so much noise that they often wake the sleeping children. The "Boom and Chime" bands then repeat their performances on Christmas Day. "Jankanoo Dancers" weave through the neighborhood, stopping at each house along the way to dance. They sometimes scare young children with their painted faces, unique masks, and shell-covered clothing.

The traditional Christmas Day feast features dishes produced from area crops. Around noon, families offer a blessing for the food, then enjoy roasted turkey, rice and beans cooked in coconut milk, fried plantains, potato salad, a black fruitcake (made black with burned sugar), white cakes (similar to pound cake), and *rum popo* (a drink made with eggs and nutmeg). The remainder of the day is spent in leisure.

Formerly a British colony, Belize also celebrates Boxing Day, a continuation of the nation's Christmas celebration. On Boxing Day, people recuperate from the hustle and bustle of Christmas before returning to work the following day. People enjoy playing outdoor sports; some communities sponsor horse racing and polo matches.

Dancing to calypso music is also popular, especially during the holiday celebration. Many community centers sponsor dances. Bird's Isle, a manmade peninsula, is one gathering place that features famous calypso musicians. Since families are encouraged to attend, it is not uncommon to see children, teenagers, and the elderly dancing together to reggae music. What a wonderful way to celebrate the holidays!

BIELARUS

Me VIASIOLYCH KALADAU

A FAIRY APPEARED HOLDING A BEAUTIFULLY DECORATED
TREE COVERED WITH ORNAMENTS REPRESENTING ALL THE
COLORS OF THE RAINBOW. TO REPLICATE THE FAIRY'S TREE,
PEOPLE BEGAN CONSTRUCTING GEOMETRIC SHAPES FROM
STRAW DYED IN AN ASSORTMENT OF COLORS.

This Eastern European country is rich with memorable holiday traditions. Most Bielarusians share similar holiday customs; however, the day of celebration differs depending on one's religious affiliation.

Jalinkas (Christmas trees) are decorated on Christmas Eve in accordance with an old Bielarusian legend. Hundreds of years ago, a mother and father were walking through the forest with their children, looking for just the right Christmas tree. A fairy appeared holding a beautifully decorated tree covered with ornaments representing all the colors of the rainbow. Alinka, their young daughter, excitedly called out to her mother, "Here is our *jalinka*." The delighted family told their neighbors, and the news of this miracle soon spread throughout the country. To replicate the fairy's tree, people began constructing geometric shapes from straw dyed in an assortment of colors. Today, *ubory* (the making of straw ornaments) is an art form, which takes a great amount of skill and patience to master.

Christmas Eve is the most religious evening of the year. In celebration of Christ's birth, the mother prepares a great feast. Sweet-smelling hay is spread on the dinner table and is covered with a white cloth. In memory of the Lord's twelve Apostles, she prepares twelve dishes in advance. Not until the first star appears in the sky can the family sit down to say the "Our Father" prayer and exchange best wishes with each other. Most families begin the meal with *kuccia* (a barley dish) and thank the Lord for the year's crops. Once they eat the *kuccia*, the family enjoys a crusty loaf of rye bread, herring, and a colorful dish of *vinihret* (beets, cucumbers, peas, green onion, and apples in a creamy mayonnaise dressing). Mushroom soup or *borsch* (beet soup), baked fish, mashed or boiled potatoes, white beans, fruit compote, *kalachi* (baked pastries filled with apricots or prunes), and *vareniki* (cheese- or cabbage-filled pastries similar to pierogis) follow and are washed down with a glass of smooth, sweet poppy seed milk. Alcoholic beverages are not permitted during the Christmas Eve supper.

Stranded travelers are always welcome to share this delicious meal. After supper, families and the weary traveler sing Christmas carols and have great fun predicting the future. The adults pull out pieces of hay from under the tablecloth to find out what next year will hold. Young ladies play games to predict who will marry next year. One such game involves grain and a rooster. After making small piles of grain in the house, the girls will bring in a rooster from the outside. A girl will be married next year if the rooster chooses her pile of grain from all the others.

Before the Bielarusian Catholics attend midnight church service, they dress in their finest clothes and anticipate a visit from traveling carolers who collect money for the poor. The hostess invites the cold carolers inside the warm house and serves them sausages, tea, warm milk, and cookies. Byzantine Orthodox families attend a liturgy on Christmas Day and enjoy the carolers in the afternoon and night.

CANADA

JOYEUX NOËL

ON THE FIRST THURSDAY IN DECEMBER, AT EXACTLY THE SAME TIME, THOUSANDS OF BRIGHT BULBS LIGHT UP THE GOVERNMENTAL BUILDINGS ACROSS THE COUNTRY. FOR THE ENTIRE CHRISTMAS SEASON, THE BUILDINGS REMAIN LIGHTED AS A REMINDER OF UNITY.

Canada is considered a mosaic of peoples. Christmas celebrations in this North American country are influenced by different ethnic backgrounds as varied as its diverse population.

Regardless of how different cultures throughout Canada celebrate the holidays, the "Lights Across Canada" ceremony attempts to unite all provinces. On the first Thursday in December, at exactly the same time, thousands of bright bulbs light up the governmental buildings across the country. For the entire Christmas season, the buildings remain lighted as a reminder of unity.

There are so many ways to celebrate during the holiday season. French Canadians in the New Brunswick, Ontario, Quebec, and Manitoba Provinces have adopted the Christmas traditions practiced in France. After Midnight Mass, in the wee hours of Christmas morning, families break the fast with the *réveillon*, a meatless yet splendid supper. Dishes served at the *réveillon* include *cretons* (pâté), *soupe aux pois* (whole pea soup), and *pudding chômeur* (maple sugar pudding cake). Children are eager for *Pere Noël's* arrival on Christmas Eve and make great efforts to be good. They receive gifts from this genial old man who visits in the hours before dawn. Others in Canada receive their presents from Santa Claus, dressed brightly in red.

The Acadians, a bilingual group who live in Nova Scotia, southern New Brunswick, and Prince Edward Island, put their own spin on their predominately French Canadian Christmas. They also enjoy a *réveillon*; however, their main course features *Pot A* (rabbit pie). Acadian children are extra careful about saying their prayers during the weeks before Christmas. Just before school lets out for the holidays, in an act of love, they decorate Christmas cards for their parents and write special messages, detailing all the prayers they have said.

During the twelve days of Christmas, Scottish Canadians enjoy *mumming*. This tradition, especially popular in Newfoundland, occurs when families or friends disguise themselves in odd-looking clothing and cover their faces so as not to be identified. They march through the streets, demanding entrance into the homes of loved ones. Once in the home, they wildly sing and dance about, disguising their voices so that the host family has no idea who the visitors are. If and when the host guesses the identity of the intruders, the *mummers* show their faces and act normally. Treated to a warm drink, they are on their way to repeat the performance at someone else's house.

After the Christmas rush, people look forward to Boxing Day, December 26. Boxing Day gets its name from an old custom of giving. Employers would present Christmas boxes made of earthenware to their servants the day after Christmas. Money was hidden inside the box, and the only way to retrieve it was to smash the box to bits. Today, Boxing Day is spent recuperating from the holidays and visiting with family and friends. Some families box up old clothes to give to the needy, while children go door to door collecting money for charity.

No matter how families celebrate the holiday season, these unique traditions unite families and communities and strengthen national pride.

CHINA

SUN TAN KWAI LA

KUNG HO HSIN HAI

THE TREES ARE NOT ONLY DECORATED WITH HOLLY, TINSEL,
AND LIGHTS, BUT WITH ORNAMENTS REPRESENTATIVE OF
CHINA'S ANCIENT CULTURE, SUCH AS COLORFUL PAPER CHAINS,
FLOWERS, LANTERNS, WOVEN RIBBON FISH, AND *Feng Huang.*

Most of China's Christmas traditions are fairly new, recently adopted from the United States and Europe after China opened to the West. In a short amount of time, Christmas quickly has become a popular holiday, although Buddhism and Taoism are the major religions of China's vast population. Because Christmas falls around the great Chinese New Year celebration, many non-Christians celebrate the Yuletide strictly as a secular holiday.

Big cities have embraced heartily many western Christmas traditions. The business districts hold ceremonies to flood the trees, windows, and streets with an extraordinary amount of colored lights. Although people who work in the cities receive the day off for Christmas, most people living in remote villages and towns are just vaguely aware of Christmas and do not celebrate it.

Lighting handcrafted paper lanterns and decorating "trees of light" (Christmas trees) are becoming popular customs. The trees, usually artificial, are not only decorated with holly, tinsel, and lights, but with ornaments representative of China's ancient culture, such as colorful paper chains, flowers, lanterns, woven ribbon fish, and *Feng Huang* (the mythical Phoenix, emperor of all birds).

Practicing Christians attend Midnight Mass on Christmas Eve. The Mass has become so popular that churches are standing-room-only. In fact, it is not uncommon for people to flow out of the churches and into the streets. Popular Christmas carols have been translated into Chinese, bringing great meaning to the beautiful songs of the season. Before bed on Christmas Eve, the family will place lighted candles in the windows for Mary and Joseph to see in the night. In some families, children hang up stockings made from muslin cloth in hopes that *Sun Ten Lao Ren* (Santa Claus) will fill them with goodies.

On Christmas Day, people who have accepted this western tradition exchange gifts. Elaborate gifts such as jewelry and silks are given to immediate family, while friends, neighbors, and distant relatives receive flowers or food. The family sits down together to enjoy a special dinner featuring all the family's favorite foods. Since the oven is not a popular appliance, many families eat fried chicken, an adaptation of the traditional turkey dinner. For this meal, fruitcakes and cookies are purchased specially from the bakery.

The major hotels in the cities throw huge parties, usually on Christmas Eve night. Young adults dress up and go to the elegant hotels to enjoy a traditional American Christmas dinner. After dinner, the hotels' dance floors open, and the party goers dance the night away in celebrations similar to America's New Year's Eve bashes.

Even though the Christmas celebration is a relatively recent addition to China's culture, the emotions the holiday evokes are nothing new. Christmas in China is celebrated as a fun and merry time, which lightens moods and lifts spirits. It is a time for friends and family to join together, dance, and celebrate the joyous season.

COLOMBIA

FELIZ NAVIDAD

DECORATING CHRISTMAS TREES IS POPULAR IN COLOMBIA.
DECORATIONS INCLUDE HANDCRAFTED FABRIC DOLLS, LITTLE BASKETS
FILLED TO THE BRIM WITH CANDY, RIBBONS, AND TOYS.

The Colombian Christmas is one of the most religious holidays of the year, filled with traditions enjoyed nationwide. The season begins on December 16, the first day of the *Novena*, and ends on January 6 with the Epiphany. During the warm winter weather, children are on a long, two-month vacation. Not having school responsibilities lends itself to celebrating Christmas to the fullest.

The *Novena* lasts for nine days, ending on Christmas Eve. Family and friends get together and pray the *Novena*. Each person takes a turn reading passages, which describe the nine days before Jesus was born. In between the narratives, the people joyously sing Christmas carols, accompanied by the festive jangle of the tambourine.

Great importance is placed upon the *pesebre* (nativity scene), which serves as the location for the *Novenas*. Families set up the *pesebre*, building a village around it, usually imitating the rustic scene of the desert. Some *pesebres*, however, are very elaborate and take up one entire room. In addition to the traditional figurines of the Holy Family and the Magi, some *pesebres* include modern amenities such as amusement parks and airports. During the season, families invite their friends and neighbors to admire their *pesebres* and open their windows for strangers to peek inside and view their elaborate creations.

Decorating Christmas trees is also popular. Because living trees are protected by the Colombian government, families enjoy decorating artificial trees or real trees potted in planters. Decorations include handcrafted fabric dolls, little baskets filled to the brim with candy, ribbons, and toys.

Christmas Eve is the climax of the Christmas season. Colombians attend Midnight Mass in beautiful summer-like weather. After Mass, a midnight feast is served, including *tamales* (chicken, sausage, and vegetables surrounded in corn flour and wrapped in plantain leaves), *natilla* (firm custard), fritters, cookies, roasted pork, bread, *ajiaco* (a rich and delicious chicken soup), and creamy hot chocolate. Once the feast is over, it is not uncommon to exchange gifts, which miraculously appear at the foot of the children's beds on Christmas Day. In Colombia, boys and girls receive gifts from Jesus, not Santa Claus.

On Christmas Day, children dress in traditional Colombian folk outfits. Little girls wear white blouses, black skirts decorated with colored ribbon, and shoes made from straw and cloth. Boys wear shirts and trousers complete with *carriels* (masculine-type purses worn across the body). Before attending a special children's Mass, boys and girls bring gifts to church for those less fortunate. Once Mass is over, the family enjoys a Christmas dinner of *paella* (a rice dish cooked with meat, seafood, and vegetables), turkey, and *buñuelos* (deep-fried, soft cheese puffs). The rest of the holiday is spent in the warmth, not only in climate, but in the heart and spirit as well.

CROATIA

SRETAN BOZIC

THE CHRISTMAS TREE HOLDS A PLACE OF PROMINENCE
IN THE CROATIAN HOME. TRADITIONALLY DECORATED ON CHRISTMAS
EVE, THE TREE IS ADORNED WITH PAINTED WALNUTS AND
ACORNS, PAPER CHAINS, DOLLS, AND PAINTED, HEART-SHAPED
ORNAMENTS HANDCRAFTED FROM BREAD DOUGH.

Croatian children eagerly anticipate the beginning of the holiday season with St. Nicholas' arrival on the evening of December 5. Boys and girls carefully place their shoes on their bedroom windowsills, hoping Saint Nicholas will visit in the night. While the children are fast asleep, St. Nicholas fills their shoes with small presents, fruit, and candy.

Housewives begin holiday preparations on Saint Lucia Day, December 13. They plant grain in water bowls to make fresh blades of sprouted grass. By Christmas Eve, the bowls show signs of young, fresh sprouts. This new greenery is placed under the family's Christmas tree and used as a centerpiece on the dining room table next to a candle and a loaf of bread.

The Christmas tree holds a place of prominence in the Croatian home. Traditionally decorated on Christmas Eve, the tree is adorned with painted walnuts and acorns, paper chains, dolls, and painted, heart-shaped ornaments handcrafted from bread dough.

The faithful believe that angels sweep down from the sky on Christmas Eve and touch springs of water with their feathery wings. This purified water is valued in Croatian homes, and on Christmas day, water is drawn from the spring with great ceremony. The water is used to make Christmas cakes and to bless the home and stables. A container of the water is kept in the home to be used throughout the year.

Christmas Eve is an all-night affair. Families attend Midnight Mass and then visit relatives after the service, singing Christmas carols while walking from home to home. The *kola*, or ring dance, is also a traditional way to celebrate the holidays. The Christmas Eve banquet is served after Mass. *Krvaica* (blood sausage) is the main course.

Early in the morning on Christmas Day, the family wakes to delicious smells coming from the oven. The mother has risen early to bake *orehnjaca* (walnut roll). Although *orehnjaca* is traditionally served for the Christmas dinner, it takes every ounce of the mother's energy to keep anxious hands from snatching tastes of this delicious bread still warm from the oven. So valued is this recipe, it is solemnly passed down from mother to daughter when she leaves home to wed. At last, the meal is served, and the family sits down to eat the scrumptious *orehnjaca*, along with roast pork and stuffed cabbage.

The rich traditions, lovingly passed down through the generations, keep families close and young at heart.

CZECH REPUBLIC

VESELÉ VÁNOCE

THE CHRISTMAS TREE PROUDLY STANDS, COVERED TOP TO BOTTOM WITH APPLES, PEARS, AND GILDED WALNUTS, FOODS THAT IN THE PAST WERE AVAILABLE ONLY DURING THE HOLIDAY SEASON.

The Christmas spirit is highly contagious. No one is immune from feeling an overwhelming sense of love, joy, and goodwill. The holiday season begins the Monday after Thanksgiving and, for some traditionalists, does not end until the Twelfth Night when the last dance is danced and the ornaments are removed from the Christmas tree.

As Saint Nicholas Day approaches, children eagerly wait for *Svatý Mikaláš* (Saint Nicholas) to descend from heaven on a golden cord. Wearing a bishop's vestments and a tall miter on his head, *Svatý Mikaláš* is a stately figure. He is followed by an angel draped in gleaming white robes and the Devil, who does not tolerate bad behavior from any child. Those who see the trio instantly fall to their knees and pray, knowing that *Svatý Mikaláš* will give good boys and girls apples, candy, and nuts from his basket. At all costs, children want to prevent the grumbling Devil from chasing them with his rattling chains.

Preparation for Christmas is almost as much fun as the day itself. During the cold wintery days, the kitchen is kept snug and warm while baking *vánočka* (sweet braided bread) and other good things to eat. Christmas is not complete without displaying the family's nativity scene. The father sits by the fire, spending many hours patiently carving new figures for the scene. The children delight in adding the new figurines to the family's beloved manger scene. Nearby, the Christmas tree proudly stands, covered top to bottom with apples, pears, and gilded walnuts, foods that in the past were available only during the holiday season. Glass ornaments, fragrant gingerbread, gilded pine cones, and delicately crocheted snowflakes also adorn the tree.

In preparation for the traditional Christmas Eve supper, the family fasts all day. The fast is broken in the evening as soon as the first star appears in the sky. Once the delicious meal is over, the grandmother shares the scraps with the outdoor animals. It is believed that the horses will become stronger, the cows will give more milk, and the chickens will lay more eggs. Burying fish bones under the fruit trees encourages the trees to bear more fruit. Even the table crumbs are thrown in the fire to prevent it from causing any harm.

The entire family gathers around the Christmas tree to spend the rest of the evening joyously singing carols and dancing. As midnight approaches, families fill the street and slowly walk to church in the quiet of the night for the Christmas Mass. Afterwards, home again, children often sleep on a hay-covered floor to experience how Jesus spent His first night on earth.

As Christmas time in the Czech Republic comes to a close, people from all over the land know in their hearts that this is a special time of joy and peace for all.

DENMARK

Merry Glaedelig Jul

Almost a century ago, Denmark gave the world the Christmas seal. These decorative stamps, depicting a variety of winter scenes, are placed on Christmas cards and packages.

Christmas in Denmark is a time for giving. Although the country shares many similar Christmas traditions with its Scandinavian neighbors, there are many aspects to the Danish Christmas season that make it unique. Both the distinctive and the shared traditions make Denmark a truly special place to be during the holidays.

Almost a century ago, Denmark gave the world the Christmas seal. These decorative stamps, depicting a variety of winter scenes, are placed on Christmas cards and packages. The Christmas seals appeared in 1903 and were so popular that other nations from around the world adopted the cause. This idea, inspired by the generosity of one Danish postal worker, created an invaluable tradition that not only supports the prevention of tuberculosis but brings out the true meaning of the holiday season.

Denmark is also responsible for the tradition of collecting the popular *Jule Aften* (Christmas Eve plates). During the holidays in earlier times, employers would give carved plates filled with pastries to their devoted servants. Not having many worldly goods, the servants collected these plates, using them for wall decorations. As time went on, the carved plates evolved into the more elaborate and highly collectible *Jule Aften*. Each year, a new plate is issued, featuring a Danish Christmas scene. The tradition of breaking the plates' molds on Christmas Eve makes these plates all the more valuable.

Following similar Scandinavian traditions, it is customary to treat birds to a tasty holiday meal. Shocks of wheat and suet are hung outside for birds to enjoy. Children and adults alike find it an enjoyable pastime to watch from the windows as the birds gobble their grain.

Families also enjoy a great feast immediately following Christmas Eve church services. After the main course of goose, members of the family enjoy looking in their dishes of rice pudding for a single almond. Finding it means good luck for the year!

Once the meal is over, the father will sneak to the Christmas tree and light the white candles. Children must wait until this time to see the tree in all its glory. Handmade ornaments cover every branch. Doves, stars, woven heart-shaped baskets filled with treats, red cornucopia, and delicate little hand muffs complement the garland of the national Danish flag. Danes believe that their flag was a gift from God. Hundreds of years ago, while out to sea, Vikings received the red and white flag in their arms as it floated down to them from heaven.

Before climbing into bed, children prepare for *Julemanden's* (Santa's) visit. *Julemanden* wears a red velvet outfit and has red wooden shoes on his feet. He travels with *Julenisser*, mischievous little elves who help deliver gifts. Children must give the *Julenisser* food and shelter so they won't create havoc by tipping over the Christmas tree or stealing the tree ornaments. Before bed, children leave saucers of milk and rice pudding for the elves and are thrilled when, in the morning, every bit of pudding and milk is gone!

ECUADOR

FELIZ NAVIDAD

IT IS GREAT FUN DECORATING LIVE EVERGREEN TREES.
DOLLS ARE DRESSED IN BEAUTIFUL HAND-SEWN GARMENTS
REPRESENTING TRADITIONAL ECUADORIAN COSTUMES, AND *Mazipan*
ORNAMENTS, MADE FROM BREAD DOUGH, ARE SHAPED, BAKED,
AND GLAZED TO LAST THROUGHOUT THE YEARS.

The holiday season begins with a flurry of activity, beginning with nine days of *novenas* (house tours). Nine days before Christmas, people, especially those who live in small towns and villages, visit their neighbors to admire the homemade mangers and nativity scenes that are erected for the occasion. Families go from house to house singing and praying, admiring the handiwork that went into the displays.

In some families, it is customary to dress up like gypsies. The littlest gypsy is given the honor of carrying a basket decorated with rose petals and flowers. The basket holds a baby doll dressed like the Christ Child. As the gypsies arrive for the *novenas*, people peek into the basket, admiring the special baby inside. Then everyone is off to the town square for a large celebration. *Empanadas* (crispy meat-filled dough similar to ravioli), traditionally eaten after the *novenas*, make the party all the more festive.

Besides decorating nativity scenes, it also is great fun decorating live evergreen trees. Dolls are dressed in beautiful hand-sewn garments representing traditional Ecuadorian costumes. *Mazipan* ornaments, made from bread dough, are shaped, baked, and glazed to make long-lasting ornaments. Handwoven hats, baskets, and other straw ornaments are popular tree ornaments, though not exclusively used just for Christmas. The straw decorations are used throughout the year; each festive occasion is identified by the color of the straw.

Families attend Midnight Mass on Christmas Eve and then visit the homes of friends and family. Before Mass, children carefully prepare letters for *Papa Noël*. They place these letters in a pair of shoes and set them out for the giving father to find, hoping that *Papa Noël* will grant their wishes. On Christmas morning, sleepy-headed children tumble out of bed to find their shoes filled with gifts.

Christmas is a day for visiting family and friends. During these visits, people indulge in tasty *pristinos* (maple syrup cookies). These cookies are a special treat reserved for this very special occasion. Christmas dinner consists of family favorites including tamales and roasted pork.

As the old year comes to an end, people dress up as clowns to greet the New Year in a happy spirit. Old clothing is stuffed to form a dummy, which is burned to usher out the old year and welcome in the new. With the New Year ahead, old acquaintances and strangers alike happily wish others well and look forward to a new beginning with countless possibilities.

EGYPT

JOYEUX NOËL

EED MELAD SA'ID

SIX WEEKS BEFORE NEW YEAR'S EVE, THE FAMILY
PLANTS FAVA BEANS, LENTILS, AND WHEAT SEEDS IN A LARGE,
COTTON-LINED TRAY. THEN WHEN SPROUTS APPEAR, THEY ARE
USED TO DECORATE DIFFERENT ROOMS IN THE HOME.

It rarely rains during the mild Yuletide season in this African country. In most areas in Egypt, the ground is bare and brown, with very few trees and very little green. To prepare for Christmas, celebrated on January 7, Coptic Christians observe Advent with a strict forty-day fast. During this time, members of this Orthodox church refrain from eating in the morning hours and eliminate meat, poultry, and dairy products from their diets.

Six weeks before New Year's Eve, the family plants fava beans, lentils, and wheat seeds in a large, cotton-lined tray. By the New Year, sprouts appear, bringing a refreshing green into the home, a sharp contrast to the brown of outdoors. The tray, separated into smaller sections, is used to decorate different rooms in the home.

The *crèche*, also an important home decoration, is often handmade in a simple design to match the simplicity of Jesus' birth in Bethlehem. The more ornate nativities of Europe are not readily available in Egypt. Families take great delight in replicating Jesus' humble beginnings by sprinkling paint on brown paper to use as a background to the *crèche*.

On Christmas Eve, everyone dresses in a brand-new outfit and sets out for church. A great ringing of bells at midnight signifies the end of the church service and the beginning of Christmas. As people file out of the church, they go home to a large meal, which breaks their forty-day fast. *Fatta* (a bread, rice, and beef dish flavored with garlic) served with pita bread; *buftake* (breaded mint-flavored veal cutlets); and rice with pecans, pine nuts, and raisins are traditional Christmas dishes. One can imagine how rich, filling, and delicious these foods taste after the long fast.

Content and full, children are sent to bed. The tired boys and girls obediently climb into bed because they know the kind and gentle *Papa Noël* cannot climb through the window until everyone is fast asleep. Children have never seen *Papa Noël*, and they do not know what he looks like. They leave him a plate of *Kahk* (shortbread sweetened with honey and cinnamon) and a glass of milk, just the same, to thank him in advance for the gifts he will leave. On Christmas morning, the boys and girls see that *Papa Noël* has left them tops, tea sets, and blocks, all toys to exercise their growing imaginations.

When the family awakens on Christmas morning, for the first time in over a month they sit down to drink hot tea with milk and nibble on feta cheese. Once breakfast is over, it is time to visit friends and relatives, at which time they exchange boxes of cookies and the warmest wishes this glorious season has to offer.

FINLAND

Hauskaa Joulua

A few days prior to Christmas, each family gathers
together to carefully choose its Christmas tree. It is
carried home and decorated the morning of Christmas Eve.

Christmas is not only a celebration of Jesus' birthday, it also represents a time of light and warmth during winter's dark and cold days. The Christmas season begins on the first Sunday of Advent. Neighbors gather at churches to hear moving Christmas music such as Vogler's "Hosanna." Children count the days before Christmas on their Advent calendars, while adults count each Sunday of Advent with candles.

A few days prior to Christmas, each family gathers together to carefully choose its Christmas tree. It is carried home and decorated the morning of Christmas Eve. Various adornments, including national flags, gingerbread cookies, and skillfully crafted handmade straw ornaments, hang on the tree branches. Dozens of candles, placed carefully on the branches, are lit for the first time on Christmas Eve night.

In preparation for Christmas Eve activities, the house has been scrubbed thoroughly. At sundown, before dressing in their best outfits, the family members take a cleansing *sauna* (steam bath). They sit down for a meal of lut fish, a giant ham, turnips, herring salad, *torttuja* (prune tarts), and a dish of rice pudding. One lucky person will find an almond in his or her serving of pudding and can anticipate good luck for the upcoming year.

Also on Christmas Eve, families visit the graveyards. They place candles on their relatives' graves and on the tombstones of soldiers who lost their lives during war. Graveyards in Finland are a wondrous sight on Christmas Eve. Thousands of glittering candles light up the dark sky, a tribute to those who are dear.

In Finland, *Joulupukki* (Father Christmas) pays a visit to children in their homes. The bearded *Joulupukki* wears a long-haired fur coat, fur hat, and big fur boots to keep his feet warm in the snow. His tiny elf assistants wear tiny gray coats, red boots, and red caps. During his visit, children have to earn their gifts by reciting poems or singing songs. Performing in front of such an imposing figure is often quite intimidating.

Christmas morning is spent in church, with the remainder of the day spent quietly with family. During the day, families reflect upon the true meaning of Christmas and strive to bring about "peace on earth, goodwill towards men."

The day after Christmas, Tapani Day, is a day of merriment. Especially in the countryside, the day is spent riding horse-drawn sleighs heavily adorned with thick strings of sleigh bells. Neighbors often race with each other to see whose sleigh is the fastest. Tapani Day is spent visiting and playing games, a welcome break from the long winter.

FRANCE

JOYEUX NOËL

FAMILIES DECORATE CHRISTMAS TREES WITH COLORED GLASS BULBS,
DOLLS DRESSED IN TRADITIONAL FRENCH DRESS, AND GARLAND.
CHILDREN ENJOY LEAVING EMPTY SPOTS ON THE TREE IN HOPES THAT
Père Noël WILL LEAVE THEM EXTRA PRESENTS IN THE SPACES.

At the beginning of the Christmas season, families in this Western European country gather together and painstakingly decorate their homes. Serving as the focal point for the French Christmas, a *crèche* (nativity scene) is set up in an area of prominence, away from the other decorations. Treasured manger figures called *santons*, or little saints, are featured in many of the *crèches*. The *santons* are handcrafted clay figurines representing different French occupations. The *crèche* is a cherished belonging, often handed down through the generations. Baskets of fruit are placed on the hearth along with candles, a French symbol of hope. Boughs of holly, garlands, and mistletoe are hung in the home to enhance a sense of natural beauty.

The Christmas tree is not as popular a tradition as in some countries. However, some families do decorate Christmas trees with colored glass bulbs, dolls dressed in traditional French dress, and garland. Children enjoy leaving empty spots on the tree in hopes that *Père Noël* (Father Christmas) will leave them extra presents in the spaces.

The Yule log is more traditional, particularly in rural areas. In earlier times, choosing the Yule log was a family affair. Entire families would walk to the forest to cut down a tree. The tree was carried home with great ceremony by the men. After cutting a log from the tree, by tradition, they would march around the living room three times and heave the log into the fireplace. Singing Christmas carols, they would pour wine over the log. However, as homes modernized, fireplaces have disappeared. The Yule log is now commonly replaced by a sponge cake shaped like a log, called *bûche de Noël*.

Anticipated by all, the *réveillon* is the traditional Christmas Eve meal, served after Midnight Mass and shared by family and friends. *Réveillon* symbolizes the holy awakening to the significance of the birth of Christ. The grandest meal of the year, the *réveillon* has many courses, which vary from region to region. This meal may consist of, depending on the region, oysters on the half shell, lobster, *pâté*, roasted goose or turkey, French cheeses, wine, and the *bûche de Noël* spread with butter or chestnut cream filling and covered with rich chocolate.

After the meal, children place their best shoes on the windowsill or near the fireplace in hopes that *Père Noël* will fill the shoes with goodies. In France, Jesus sends the red-robed *Père Noël* to children's homes. Boys and girls enjoy leaving a snack for him, as well as for his donkey. As hard as the children wish for a visit from *Père Noël*, they wish just as hard for his helper to stay away. *Le Père Fouettard* (Father Spanker) has been known to drag naughty children out of bed, during a sound sleep, for a spanking. Very early on Christmas morning, children open the presents left by *Père Noël*. Lucky children receive gifts not only in their shoes, but on the tree as well. Once again, the kind-hearted *Père Noël* prevailed earning the loyalty of countless children throughout the land.

GERMANY

FRÖHLICHE WEINACHTEN

SOME CREDIT MARTIN LUTHER WITH CREATING THE FIRST
LIGHTED CHRISTMAS TREE. LEGEND HAS IT THAT WHILE WALKING
HOME ONE EVENING THROUGH THE SNOWY FOREST,
MARTIN LUTHER NOTICED STARLIGHT FILTERING THROUGH
A BEAUTIFUL, SNOW-COVERED FIR TREE.

Festivities and fun are essential to Germany's six-week Christmas season. Friends, family, and neighbors visit, exchange presents, and enjoy the season's rich foods. The celebration begins on Saint Andrew's Night, November 30, a time for young girls to dream of their future husbands. The Christmas season ends on the Octave of Epiphany, January 13. On this day, young boys, dressed as the Three Kings, march the streets reenacting their journey to see the Christ Child.

German children anticipate a visit from Saint Nicholas, the patron saint of children, on December 6. Saint Nicholas does not have reindeer. Instead, a snow-white pony helps him carry two bags. One bag is filled with presents for good boys and girls, while the other is filled with switches for the naughty. On this children's holiday, young and old alike enjoy eating gingerbread cookies.

Some credit Martin Luther with creating the first lighted Christmas tree. Legend has it that while walking home one evening through the snowy forest, Martin Luther noticed starlight filtering through a beautiful, snow-covered fir tree. To him the glistening tree was heaven. Wanting to share the beauty of that tree with his wife and children, he cut it down and strung white candles on it to recreate the breathtaking vision he saw in the forest.

On Christmas Eve, December 24, parents light the gleaming *tannenbaum* (Christmas tree) for their children to enjoy. Parents decorate the tree with white candles and handblown glass ornaments. Germany was the first country to hang glass ornaments from the tree. The last ornament hung on the tree is a pickle. The parents carefully hide the pickle among the tree branches. As the tree is presented to the children, they scurry around the tree hunting for the pickle. The lucky child observant enough to find the pickle among the green branches gets a special gift left by Saint Nicholas. Additionally, a nativity scene depicting the birth of Baby Jesus is displayed proudly in most German homes. Family and friends gather to sing Christmas carols such as "Oh Tannenbaum," exchange gifts, and partake in the delicious foods of the season, including carp, the traditional Christmas Eve dish. Attending a midnight church service completes the Christmas Eve celebration.

Christmas Day is spent quietly at home among family. Relatives may come calling to exchange gifts and admire the decorated tree. The traditional Christmas menu includes roasted goose, *spätzle* (noodle dough), *pfersnüssen* (pepper nut balls), and *swarzwalder chentorte* (black forest cherry cake). Pleasantly full, adults take the time to visit instead of rushing off after dinner. Older children play good-natured games with younger children until it is time to scamper off to bed. Snuggled in a warm bed, children bask in the true spirit of Christmas.

GREECE

Me Kala Christougena

Christmas Day is spent attending an early morning church
service. The remainder of the day is spent visiting with family
and friends, enjoying good company and delicious food.

Christmas in Greece is an important holiday celebrated with a great sense of family and community. Singing and dancing are an integral part of the holiday festivities. On Christmas Eve, children gather together and sing *kalandas*, songs similar to Christmas carols. The *kalandas* often are accompanied by the ringing of triangles and the beating of small clay drums. The children are rewarded for a job well done with sweets and dried fruit.

A great feast is served on Christmas Day. Traditional dishes served at this meal include a roast leg of lamb and sweet loaves of bread called *christopsomo* (Christ bread). The baker of the bread forms the loaves that relate to the family's profession. *Kourambiedes* (powdered sugar cookies), a Christmas favorite, are served for dessert. Each cookie is studded with a clove to symbolize the gift of spices the Wise Men brought to Baby Jesus. These yummy cookies are a holiday favorite, and children come back again and again for additional helpings.

Christmas Day is spent attending an early morning church service. The remainder of the day is spent visiting with family and friends, enjoying good company and delicious food.

On Saint Basil's Day, January 1, the family joins once again for a special meal, which begins with a sponge cake called *Vasilopeta*. A cross, formed with dough, adorns the top of the loaf, and with a knife, a cross is cut on the bottom. The father slices off the first piece in honor of Jesus. The second slice is for the blessing of the family's home. The next slice is set aside for the poor, while the remaining pieces are passed to the family members according to age, oldest to youngest. As the family members accept their pieces of bread, they look to see if theirs has a silver coin in it. Good luck and prosperity come to the person who finds the coin. Once the bread is sliced, the rest of the meal can be enjoyed.

A moving ritual is suitable for the end of the holiday season. After church services on the Epiphany, parishioners and priests gather on the banks of a local spring or river for the "Blessing of the Waters" ceremony to commemorate Jesus' baptism in the River Jordan. A symbol of the Holy Spirit, a captured white dove, is released as a priest throws a cross in the water. Young men jump in the water to rescue the cross. Much honor is given to the man who rescues the cross, so competition is often intense, and much splashing ensues. The person who retrieves the cross receives a special blessing. Afterwards, people approach the water to fill their containers to be placed near their holy icons at home. The act of throwing a cross in the water is believed to drive back evil spirits; to complete the cleansing, the local priest calls on homes to bless them with holy water, ensuring that every evil spirit is banished.

GUATEMALA

FELIZ NAVIDAD

Nacimientos ARE FOUND IN EVERY HOME AND CHURCH. MOST
HOMES PLACE THE TRADITIONAL NATIVITY FIGURINES IN FRONT
OF A BACKGROUND MADE TO LOOK LIKE BETHLEHEM.

Guatemala's Christmas celebration starts on December 16 with much ceremony. The festivities continue until the Epiphany on January 6. The beginning of this three-week celebration centers around the *posada*, a reenactment of Joseph and Mary's search for shelter.

Before this nine-day procession begins, people in villages all around Guatemala anticipate the ceremonial beating of turtle shells. The hollow thunking sound the shells produce announces that Joseph and Mary are seeking shelter. On behalf of Joseph and his wife, villagers go from home to home asking for a place to rest. Time and again, the villagers are turned out. Finally, at the end of the evening, a hospitable family accepts the travelers, who shout with joy. Although Joseph and Mary must live among ox and ass, the participants feel relief that the couple can rest safely at last.

The evening's host treats his wearied guests to *punche* (a warm tea flavored with dried fruit and cinnamon). This drink is welcomed with pleasure since December evenings can become quite cool. The *posadas* repeat for nine nights until Christmas Eve, when the biggest and most important *posada* takes place. Hosting the *posada* on Christmas Eve is quite an honor. The host family carefully prepares for the festival of the *Nacimiento* (crèche). At the end of the Christmas Eve *posada*, the procession carefully places the Baby Jesus in his manger of the *Nacimiento*.

Nacimientos are found in every home and church. Most homes place the traditional nativity figurines in front of a background made to look like Bethlehem. However, in other homes, erecting the *Nacimientos* can become quite a production. Some *Nacimientos* take weeks to build and take up an entire room. Many create *Nacimientos* representing the culture by replicating Guatemala's landscape. The figurines are carved to look like local villagers.

After Baby Jesus is placed in his manger on the last night of the *posada*, the procession moves to the local church for a stirring Midnight Mass. After Mass, children take turns striking a *piñata*, hoping that their accurate swings will produce a hail of candy, nuts, and small toys. On this special night, boys and girls are allowed to stay awake to see a great fireworks display. After the family watches the last bright burst of color fill the midnight sky, the family opens presents and then sits down to eat *tamales*, a Christmas Eve treat most families can't do without.

HAWAII

MELE KALIKIMAKA A ME
HAU'OLI MAKAHIKI HOU

BEFORE THE ISLANDS HAD CONTACT WITH THE OUTSIDE
WORLD, HAWAIIANS CELEBRATED *Makahiki* FROM OCTOBER
THROUGH JANUARY, IN HONOR OF THE GOD LONO.

The blending together of outside cultures makes the Hawaiian Christmas a truly diversified celebration. Many Christmas customs appear to mirror those of the Mainland; however, Hawaii has a rich history and tradition all its own.

Before the Islands had contact with the outside world, Hawaiians celebrated *Makahiki* from October through January, in honor of the god Lono. In war and in peace, any existing hostilities ceased so that the men could prove their strength and endurance in sporting contests.

Hawaii's isolation ended in January 1778, when Captain James Cook stumbled upon the Islands while trying to discover the Northwest Passage. The natives mistook Captain Cook for the god Lono because his ship's sails resembled the *kapa* cloth (strips of paper mulberry bark, wet, beaten, and designed by stamping) identified with Lono's clothing. Cook's arrival seemed to fulfill the native's prophecy that Lono would return.

Missionaries began arriving in Hawaii during the 1820s and slowly introduced the natives to Christianity. At first, Christmas was observed as a religious holiday by devoted Christians. Over time, as more ethnic groups, such as the Germans, Japanese, and Filipinos, arrived to work in Hawaii's great fields, these foreigners brought their own holiday traditions to their new home. Christmas and a variety of other winter holidays, such as *Shogatsu* (Japanese New Year), influenced how families celebrate Christmas today.

Hawaii's warm and sunny weather allows for many Christmas customs to take place outdoors. Luaus are a popular way to celebrate Christ's birth. During these informal gatherings, people enjoy the rich flavor of *Kalua* pig. This main course is accompanied by *poi* (baked kalo root pounded into paste). During these events, families also sing and dance to a variety of ancient and modern music.

Since Hawaii is surrounded by water, accommodations must be made to enjoy the traditions popular on the Mainland. Instead of arriving in Hawaii on a sleigh pulled by reindeer, Santa Claus must make the long journey from the North Pole in a red canoe. People wanting live Christmas trees must have them shipped from the northwest region of the Mainland.

Families decorate Christmas trees according to their own ethnic traditions. Great importance is placed on the nativity scene, which can have a Hawaiian theme. *Iesu* (Jesus) may be wrapped in soft *kapa* cloth and placed on finely woven mats. Instead of frankincense and myrrh, the Three Wise Men give *Iesu* gifts from the bounty of the sea or earth, such as shells, fish, seaweed, or fragrant flowers.

On the islands, families attend church services, while others may partake in the traditions passed down by their ancestors. Families may participate in the "Clearing of the Pathway," a ritual to accomplish necessary tasks of life without impediment. Still others may thank nature for the gifts of the forests and the sea. Mutual respect for the variety of celebrations keeps the holiday spirit alive.

Hungary

Boldog Karácsony

As evening falls upon the countryside, family
members gather around the beautifully decorated
Christmas tree to say a short prayer.

Hungary, located in central Europe, celebrates Christmas for two days, beginning on Christmas Eve. Much of the holiday celebration centers around the Christmas tree traditionally decorated with products of the country's bountiful harvest such as apples, pears, and nuts. Honey cookies, called *mézeskalács*, fill the air with their fragrant scent, and *Szalon cukar*, a homemade chocolate candy similar to fudge, is festively wrapped in silver foil, adding to the beauty of the tree. Embroidered heart- and slipper-shaped ornaments made from felt complete the tree's adornments.

As evening falls upon the countryside, family members gather around the beautifully decorated Christmas tree to say a short prayer. Gifts are distributed to all and are opened with great enthusiasm. Once the first star appears in the sky, the family is allowed to eat a great Christmas Eve feast. This meal traditionally is composed of many courses, including cabbage or chicken soup with liver dumplings, fruit compote, fish, and horn-shaped cakes filled with poppy seeds, apricots, or walnuts. The meat served, usually roasted chicken or duck, is chosen from the available supply out of the barnyard. Since hospitality is very important to Hungarians, it is traditional to save room at the table for a stranger who may come by seeking company on this joyous holiday. The stranger can be sure that he or she will be well fed since food is generously portioned out.

After enjoying the delicious meal, the remaining crumbs are swept from the floor by an unmarried girl. She throws the crumbs through the threshold in hopes of seeing a vision of her future husband. Afterwards, she and the rest of the family members dress in traditional Hungarian costumes and attend Midnight Mass. All members eagerly attend the church service, because, while they are gone, Saint Nicholas visits each home in the village, leaving presents for all who are good. Since the house has to be empty for Saint Nicholas to do his job, there is incentive to go to church. The church itself, usually located on top of the tallest hill in each village, is decorated with hundreds of candles, evergreens, and flowers. Also among the decorations is a nativity scene with the Holy Family, angels, the Three Kings, shepherds, and their flocks of animals.

After church, children march the streets singing Christmas carols. They often carry a tray of marionettes, figures from the nativity scene, to reenact the Christmas story for neighbors, snug in their homes, who look out windows to view the show.

At last, everyone returns home where children are allowed to open the presents left by Saint Nicholas. Exhausted from a long day of excitement, the family retires to their beds. Proud of the customs developed over countless generations, most Hungarians still practice Christmas traditions in their homes today.

ICELAND

GLEDILEG JOL

LIGHTS THROUGHOUT THE HOME ARE LEFT TO BURN
THROUGHOUT THE NIGHT AND INTO CHRISTMAS DAY TO HONOR
THE BIRTH OF THE CHRIST CHILD.

Iceland, the smallest of the Scandinavian countries, begins the holiday season on December 12, thirteen days before Christmas. People in Iceland celebrate Christmas with not one but thirteen different Santas.

According to a thirteenth-century legend, two ogres, Gryla and Leppalothi, live on the tall, snowy mountains. When her husband, Leppalothi, was bedridden, Gryla came down off the mountain and begged for food. During the Christmas season, she stole naughty children to eat. Gryla's cat was also very mean. The cat walked the countryside taking anyone who did not wear new clothes for Christmas. These folk tales so frightened the children that, in 1746, the King of Iceland (also the Danish King) forbade anyone from playing tricks on others in the spirit of these stories.

Gryla and Leppalothi had thirteen elf-like children known as *Jolasveninar* (Santa Clauses). *Jolasveninar* are good-natured, yet mischievous, little elves, not at all evil like their parents. Thirteen days before Christmas, one each day, the elves take turns coming off the mountain to enter each home in town. They leave a gift in each pair of shoes that is left out on the windowsill. Children who will not behave receive insulting presents like potatoes to remind them to be good.

Children are not afraid of the *Jolasveninar*. Rather, they look forward to their visits, regardless of their mischievous deeds. The Crevice Imp hides in corners, the Meat Hooker tries to take the roast, and the Candle Beggar steals candles. People try with all their might to keep things out of the reach of the *Jolasveninar*. Beginning on Christmas Day, the *Jolasveninar* return to their mountain home, one by one. The last elf leaves town on January 6.

On Christmas Eve, families enjoy looking at the just-decorated Christmas tree. Handmade elf ornaments made from yarn honor the *Jolasveninar*. Handmade wreaths and snowflakes, representing the Christmas snow, also bedeck the tree. Candles, made from mutton tallow, burn bright, completing the tree. Lights throughout the home are left to burn throughout the night and into Christmas Day to honor the birth of the Christ Child. Children, on this special occasion, are permitted to stay up late into the night.

Families attend church on Christmas Day and afterwards enjoy a feast of good, rich food. Family favorites include smoked *mutton* (sheep), *laufabraud* (fancy fried cakes), rock ptarmigan, and porridge. A special Christmas cake filled with currants and raisins completes the meal.

The Christmas season officially ends on New Year's Eve. People gather in the public squares and watch the great bonfires, which symbolize the breaking of the winter solstice and the return of the sun. Christmas trees and wrapping paper are added by each family to help sustain the great blaze.

INDIA

MERRY CHRISTMAS

LUXURIOUS FABRICS PROVIDE THE CHRISTMAS TREE WITH BRIGHT AND
CELEBRATORY COLORS, WHICH LEND ELEGANCE TO THE TREE.

Christmas is celebrated amid much joy and reverence. The richly contrasting colors used to decorate homes and towns are a telltale sign that Christmas is in the air. Poinsettia plants help paint the background a brilliant red, while dark mango leaves and palm fronds lend the home's interior and exterior a green hue representative of India's tropical climate.

Weeks before Christmas, young children go from door to door in their neighborhood, joyously singing Christmas carols. Their sweet voices fill the air each evening until, at last, Christmas arrives. Neighbors often stroll out of their homes to watch the children earnestly sing the Yuletide carols, feeling all the pleasant emotions this season brings.

The home itself is decorated with a *crèche*, a Christmas tree, and a special Star of Bethlehem. It is the children's job to set up the *crèche*, a responsibility they take very seriously. Weeks before, they soak seeds in water and use the sprouts to be used as background greenery for the family's *crèche*. Erecting the *crèche* provides hours of family entertainment, the results admired by appreciative parents. Because India is in a tropical area, obtaining a live fir or pine tree is impractical. Families, however, do decorate artificial trees, which replicate the traditional Christmas tree. They are decorated with beautifully handmade ornaments using readily available supplies and products of India. Palm fronds and jute rope provide a unique and natural-looking garland. Garland and decorative bows often are made from the beautiful silks and the very fine cotton gauze of a woman's *sari* (women's traditional clothing). These luxurious fabrics provide the tree with bright and celebratory colors, which lend elegance to the tree. Parents and children look forward to creating a handmade Star of Bethlehem, which hangs outside the front door and is lit from within.

Throughout the Christmas season, women are busy in the kitchen making Christmas pastries. These rich, sugary confections are made from a variety of ingredients, the most popular being coconut. Favorite Christmas treats include *naories* (fried filled pastries, the edges crimped with a fork) and *kulkuls* (fried Christmas cookies). Some mothers and daughters compete with each other to see who can fry the most *kulkuls*. Friendly games such as this make time in the kitchen pass quickly.

Midnight Mass is celebrated with much pomp and circumstance. Since Christmas Eve is such a special occasion, Mass lasts longer than normal to accommodate all the special carols and the beautiful retelling of the night Christ was born in Bethlehem. Long after Mass is over, parishioners linger in the church, wishing one and all a very Merry Christmas.

On Christmas Day, boys and girls wake up eager to open their gifts left under the Christmas tree by Santa. However, children are not allowed to open their gifts until they have eaten a good, hearty breakfast. Later in the day, families and friends visit and enjoy an elaborate dinner featuring favorite Indian dishes.

IRELAND

NODLAIG NAIT CUGAT

ON CHRISTMAS NIGHT, THE OLDEST IN THE FAMILY GATHERS
ITS MEMBERS AROUND FOR A SNUG AND WARM EVENING
OF STORYTELLING. THE EVENING BEGINS WITH THE CHRISTMAS
STORY OF MARY, JOSEPH, AND THE CHRIST CHILD.

Christmas is considered the most holy and enjoyable holiday of the year. Although anticipation builds weeks before, the twelve days of Christmas do not begin until Christmas Eve.

Weeks before Christmas, the home is scrubbed from ceiling to floor. However, many Christmas preparations are left for Christmas Eve. On that day, everyone rises early to run errands and decorate the home before the evening activities. It is not uncommon to begin shopping for Christmas gifts on this day. Lighted candles are placed in every window in every house to light the way for Mary and Joseph. The doors to homes are left open through the night. It is a breathtaking experience to go outside on Christmas Eve and climb the tallest hilltop. Looking across the village, one can see thousands of flickering lights illuminating the dark night.

The nativity scene holds a place of importance throughout the nation. Families create the manger scene by carefully placing each figurine in its proper place. The manger is left empty until Christmas Eve when the Baby Jesus is placed lovingly in his crib.

Christmas morning begins early with a grand breakfast. Christmas dinner is the most elaborate meal of the year. A ham, roasted goose, or a potato-stuffed turkey is served with a variety of vegetables and a plum pudding, made fat with raisins and currants. The Christmas cake is an absolute necessity during Christmas. Prepared in October to allow for sufficient mellowing, the cake is made from caramel, dried fruits, blanched almonds, and brandy. It is not uncommon for homes to have removable bricks within their walls to hide the cake during the mellowing process. When Christmas nears, the cake is first dunked in *marzipan* (almond paste) and then in snow white icing, which signifies purity.

On Christmas night, the oldest in the family gathers its members around for a snug and warm evening of storytelling. The evening begins with the Christmas story of Mary, Joseph, and the Christ Child. Afterwards, others join in, telling stories about ancestors and their struggles for survival. Sharing these stories builds a great sense of pride and belonging and helps to preserve Ireland's rich history.

On December 26, people look forward to Saint Stephen's Day, named after the first Christian martyr. Saint Stephen was stoned after being accused of speaking out against the Ten Commandments. It is said he was betrayed by a wren, while hiding from his enemies. The highlight of this day is the "Wren Boy Procession." Boys place a live wren in a cage and attach it to a furze bush. The children, wearing masks and elaborate costumes, visit homes asking for money, in the name of the wren. The money is then given to charity.

On Little Christmas, January 6, the Magi finally are added to complete the nativity scene. With the official end of the holiday season, many look upon this day with melancholy. Yet, throughout the year, family and friends continue to gather, reminiscing about Christmas past.

ITALY

BUON NATALE

MADE OF CLAY, GLASS, WOOD, AND OTHER MATERIALS,
THE MANGER SCENES ARE AN ART FORM AND TAKE MANY
SHAPES, FROM THE SIMPLE TO THE ORNATE.

This southern European country began celebrating Christ's birthday around 300 A.D. Since then, the Italian observation is truly a religious celebration centered around the nativity.

St. Francis of Assisi is credited for creating the nativity scene. People gathered throughout the little village of Greccio to hear Assisi tell the Christmas story. To paint a picture in the villagers' minds, he recreated the manger scene using live animals. What a sight to behold! Since then, Italians and much of the world over have adopted the *presepio* (manger scenes). Italians, especially, take great pride in crafting little figurines of the *presepio*. Made of clay, glass, wood, and other materials, the manger scenes are an art form and take many shapes, from the simple to the ornate. It is a special privilege to be present at the Vatican the Sunday before Christmas. At this time, children bring the Baby Jesus from their *presepio* for the Pope's special blessing, an honor the children treasure for a lifetime.

Christmas trees are not traditionally used during Christmas; instead, families light the Yule log. On Christmas Eve, children are blindfolded and stand near the fireplace. Each child recites a sermon to the Christ Child. Then, the blindfold is removed, and gifts appear from nowhere.

Relatives, near and far, gather together as a family on Christmas Eve. Hours before leaving for Midnight Mass, a large supper is enjoyed by all. It is traditional to eat only meatless dishes in this grand feast. Many families practice the tradition of eating an odd number of courses, which may include shrimp, a pasta with clam or anchovy sauce, deep-fried smelt, and oven-baked fish. Cod fish salad, vegetables, and dessert, such as *cannoli* (a pastry horn stuffed with cream or ricotta cheese), top off the grand feast. Once the meal ends, family members are grateful to be outdoors, breathing in the crisp air on their way to Midnight Mass. Once Mass is over, families continue to celebrate into the wee hours of the night.

On January 6, the Feast of the Epiphany, children continue to receive gifts. They hang up their stockings and wait for Befana, Italy's gift giver. It is said that on their way to Bethlehem to see the Christ Child, the Three Kings stopped at Befana's home, announcing the birth of Christ. They asked her for directions and invited her to travel with them. Preoccupied with her own concerns, she turned the Kings out. Later, she felt regret and tried with all her might to find the manger. She gathered up gifts that once belonged to her deceased child and set out for Bethlehem. However, it was too late, and she never laid eyes on the Baby Jesus. It is said that every year she hunts in vain for the Christ Child. Unable to find Him, she leaves the gifts meant for Jesus at children's homes throughout Italy.

Once the Epiphany is over, people go back to their daily routines; however, the events of the holidays are not forgotten, and the spirit of Christmas lives on and on.

LATVIA

PRIECĪGUS ZIEMSVĒTKUS

GEOMETRIC-SHAPED ORNAMENTS MADE FROM STRAW, APPLES,
AND A GARLAND MADE FROM CRANBERRIES MAKE ONE APPRECIATE
THE SIMPLE BEAUTY OF NATURE'S GIFTS.

In this Baltic state, great amounts of snow cover the ground during the holidays. The season gets underway with *Martiņi*, a tradition similar to America's Halloween. On November 10, adults and children alike dress in costumes or animal masks as *Ķekatnieki* (also known as *Budęli*). During this exciting time, everyone sings and dances from house to house. It is believed that *Ķekatnieki* can gain power over evil spirits and bestow health, happiness, fertility, and a bountiful harvest. Although this is an old pagan tradition dating back before Christ, visiting homes, while in disguise, in the name of all good things remains an important holiday activity.

In Latvia today, the tree is decorated with items found in Latvian fields. Geometric-shaped ornaments made from straw, apples, and a garland made from cranberries make one appreciate the simple beauty of nature's gifts. Before electricity, the tree was lighted with hand-dipped candles.

Children look forward for *Ziemsvētku Vecītis* (the Latvian Santa Claus) to come to their homes on Christmas Eve. Since Latvia is a relatively small country, *Ziemsvētku Vecītis* is able to visit each and every child personally. Dressed in a dark red coat, *Ziemsvētku Vecītis* has a long white beard and can be quite stern at times. He demands that the children earn their gifts by singing a song or reciting a poem. If they fail to do this simple task, *Ziemsvētku Vecītis* will spank their little bottoms with a small bundle of branches called brushwood. He gives nice gifts to obedient children and nothing but switches to the children who have been bad.

Families attend church on Christmas Eve night and Christmas morning. The rest of Christmas Day is spent casually visiting, eating, and having fun. Special foods are prepared for the three-day holiday celebration. Family favorites are *pīrāgi* (small rolls with bacon and onion filling); roast pig; and dried beans, peas, fruits, and berries preserved from the fall harvest. Adults also indulge in home-brewed beer.

Taking advantage of a full house, people often participate in folk dances and games, such as "the wolf and the goat." In this game, everyone forms a circle and sings. A person playing the wolf, a symbol of evil and darkness, tries to catch the goat, symbolizing goodness and light. The people in the circle prevent the wolf from catching his prey in a selfless act of unity.

Fortune-telling is also a creative way to pass the time. Little streams of molten lead, dropped in a bucket of water, harden into metal. Everyone must predict the future by the hardened metal shapes. If a piece resembles a horse, then that person may go riding. If a chunk looks like a suitcase, a trip is in store.

As the afternoon turns to evening and another Christmas ends, perhaps visions of future holiday seasons will bring happiness and light to all families.

LEBANON

JOYEUX NOÊL

MEELAD MAJEED

THREE WEEKS BEFORE CHRISTMAS DAY, THE FAMILY
BEGINS PLANNING FOR THE *crèche* BY PLANTING ALFALFA. AS
CHRISTMAS APPROACHES, AN ELABORATE *crèche* IS SET UP
TO LOOK LIKE A LITTLE BETHLEHEM.

Lebanon is the only Arab nation to celebrate Christmas as a national holiday. Also during this time of year, Lebanese Muslims celebrate their New Year, while the country's Jewish community observes Hanukkah. The multiple holiday celebrations make December a festive time. For this reason, the streets and shops throughout the country are decorated gaily in color and light.

Great importance is placed on the *crèche* (nativity scene), because it tells the story of the birth of Christ. Three weeks before Christmas Day, the family begins planning for the *crèche* by planting alfalfa. As Christmas approaches, an elaborate *crèche* is set up to look like a little Bethlehem. The delicate blades of alfalfa grass are used to help make the *crèche* look realistic. Soon after the *crèche* is in place, the family decorates a pine or artificial tree to their own taste, often with imported glass ornaments. Children also work hard creating live nativity scenes, which bring the Christmas story to life. Performed at churches and schools, these presentations are a favorite tradition.

On Christmas Eve, families attend Midnight Mass, where children sing special musical programs for the congregation. After returning home from Mass, children all over the country are thrilled to find that *Papa Noêl* (Santa Claus) has left them presents near the manger or under the Christmas tree. During this happy time, children also receive candy and new clothes.

Doors are open to family and friends on Christmas Day. This is a wonderful time to enjoy rich food, such as lamb, beef roast, turkey or duck, and *tabouleh* ("Lebanese supreme salad") made from cracked wheat, mint, tomatoes, parsley, and onions. A variety of tasty desserts help end the meal, including *baklawa* (flaky pastry made from phyllo dough, sugar, walnuts, and rose water) and the seasonal confection *Bûche de Noêl* (the traditional Yule log cake). Adults also enjoy Turkish coffee, a fine accompaniment for the pastries.

Homes remain open until New Year's Day. Children play together, while adults take this opportunity to catch up with one another. Guests help themselves to bowls of chestnuts, mixed nuts, imported chocolate, and Jordan almonds. Always hospitable, the hostess will not allow her guests to go home hungry. If a guest is too full to eat, which often happens after visiting several homes, the hostess will fill the guest's pockets with chocolates and other goodies. Lucky children are thrilled to help the recipient lighten his load. What a wonderful way to celebrate the birth of Christ and ring in the New Year!

LITHUANIA

LINKSMŲ KALĒDŲ

Lithuanian families use bird ornaments made from nut shells, birch bark, and feather or paper wings. Just like the boughs of the past, the Christmas tree fills the home with a fragrance that could be described only as Christmas.

The spirit of Christmas burns bright in this Eastern European country. For countless generations, families have participated in the beloved tradition which make Lithuania's Christmas celebration so charming.

Contemporary Lithuania uses Christmas trees just like many other cultures. In times past, traditional holiday decorations did not include Christmas trees. The nature-loving Lithuanians were reluctant to cut down trees, even for a special time like Christmas. Instead, families draped evergreen boughs through the living space and decorated them with materials that could have been found around Jesus' manger: straw, eggshells, feathers, nuts, and, especially, *šiaudinukai* ornaments. These intricate, geometric-shaped ornaments are made from rye or wheat straw. It takes many hours and great ingenuity to make *šiaudinukai*. The shapes of the ornaments are limited only by the maker's imagination. Although *šiaudinukai* are usually the trees' exclusive decoration, some Lithuanian families also may use bird ornaments made from nut shells, birch bark, and feather or paper wings. Just like the boughs of the past, the Christmas tree fills the home with a fragrance that could be described only as Christmas.

For the *Kucios*, the Christmas Eve meal, fresh hay is spread on the dinner table. This serves as a reminder that Jesus was born in a stable and slept in a hay-filled manger. A pure linen table cloth is placed over the hay. It is used only once during the whole year, each Christmas Eve, and is a cherished heirloom passed down from generation to generation. Lighted candles are placed upon the table as are *kalēdaitis* (Holy Christmas wafers). To honor their memory, a place is set for any family member who passed away during the year. This also is done for anyone who could not return home for the holiday. As soon as the first star appears in the sky, the father says a prayer and offers the mother a holy wafer, wishing her a Merry Christmas. Offering the father her own wafer, the mother wishes that God will keep the family together for another year. The parents offer the remaining wafers to the children and exchange happy Christmas greetings.

Christmas is especially joyous for children. They take great pleasure in tasting well water to see if it has turned into wine. On Christmas Eve night, some parents allow their children to sleep in the barn to hear for themselves if the animals will talk. Legend has it that the grateful Christ Child gives animals the power to speak on Christmas Eve because they gave him their warm manger to sleep in so many years ago. *Kaledu Senelis*, the Lithuanian Santa Claus, requires that children earn presents by singing and dancing. They receive their presents only after they perform for *Kaledu Senelis*. Later, the family attends Midnight Mass. The week between Christmas Day and New Year's Day is spent visiting, singing, and dancing. It is truly a joyous time of celebration.

LUXEMBOURG

GLÉCKLECHEN
CHRËSCHTDAG

ORNAMENTS VARY FROM HOME TO HOME; SOME FAVORITE
DECORATIONS INCLUDE THE LUXEMBOURG FLAG, RIBBONS,
AND CROCHETED SNOWFLAKE ORNAMENTS. A STAR
OF BETHLEHEM ORNAMENT TOPS THE TREE.

The holiday season begins on Saint Nicholas Day, December 6, in this tiny European country. Beginning in December, city streets and store windows are decorated with sparkling lights, while Christmas trees are placed in public squares. Saint Nicholas keeps busy pleasing the children in Luxembourg. One week before Saint Nicholas Day, children place their slippers in front of their bedroom doors, hoping that Saint Nicholas will fill them with gifts. Before bedtime on Saint Nicholas Eve, children mark plates with their names and place them on the dining room table. If they have been good all year, Saint Nicholas will cover the plates with presents and good things to eat. Children also may receive hats and mittens, which keep little heads and hands warm on cold winter days.

Although a joyous time, children dread hearing a knock on the door. This means that Black Peter is paying a visit to naughty boys and girls. Children who have been unbearably bad are strapped to Black Peter's belt and carried off in great humiliation for all the villagers to see. A visit from Black Peter almost guarantees good behavior for the next year because no little boy or girl wants to experience Black Peter's wrath twice!

Once Saint Nicholas Day is over, families set up a *crèche* depicting the night that Christ was born in a manger. Although not as popular, the practice of decorating Christmas trees is enjoyed by some families. Ornaments vary from home to home; some favorite decorations include the Luxembourg flag, ribbons, and crocheted snowflake ornaments. A Star of Bethlehem ornament tops the tree.

Christmas in Luxembourg is a religious time of reflection and reverence; therefore, many of the traditions focus on the birth of Baby Jesus. On Christmas Eve night, parents gather around the *crèche* or tree and explain to their children the meaning of Christmas. Parents stress to the children that Christmas "is a new beginning to try to do better in all things." The family sings songs in the spirit of Christmas, and each child is given an orange, a wintertime delicacy. Midnight Mass contributes meaning to this beautiful night. A special Christmas breakfast is served either immediately after Mass or after a good night's sleep.

Flavorful smoked ham and piping hot *kirmeskuch* (yeast bread) served with butter fill the home with good smells. In some areas, children put on Christmas programs for the community to enjoy. The remainder of the day is spent in earnest reflection of the true meaning of Christmas.

MEXICO

FELIZ NAVIDAD

FAMILIES TAKE GREAT PRIDE IN SETTING UP *pesebres*. THE *pesebre*
IS A HOLIDAY CENTERPIECE FOUND IN MOST MEXICAN HOMES.
RANGING FROM SIMPLE TO ELABORATE, SMALL FIGURINES ARE
SET UP TO REPRESENT THE BIRTH OF JESUS CHRIST.

The sweet scent of flowers fills the warm air during Mexico's Christmas season. Beginning December 16, Mexicans enjoy *fiestas* (parties), singing, dancing, and delicious food. Adding to the joyous atmosphere, town squares, streets, and homes are decorated in lights, bright paper lanterns, *piñatas*, poinsettias, and *pesebres* (nativity scenes).

Families take great pride in setting up *pesebres*. The *pesebre* is a holiday centerpiece found in most Mexican homes. Ranging from simple to elaborate, small figurines are set up to represent the birth of Jesus Christ. Some families also decorate Christmas trees. A variety of trees are available, including pine trees and cacti. Although decorations differ from region to region, many trees are dressed with colorful paper flowers and glass and silver ornaments.

Posadas are also a prominent Christmas ritual. From December 16 through Christmas Eve, a procession of children and adults reenacts Joseph and Mary's journey to Bethlehem. Holding lighted candles, they slowly walk the streets each evening, knocking on neighbors' doors in search of shelter. In keeping with the Bible story, all homes are closed to the weary travelers. On Christmas Eve, the last *posada* ends at church, where all involved attend Midnight Mass.

After Midnight Mass, firecrackers and other noisemakers fill the air. Families and friends return home to feast on turkey and hot chocolate (foods native to Mexico), as well as *tortillas*, fried peppers, vegetables, and a Christmas salad made from fruit, nuts, beets, and sugar cane. Before going to bed, children complete the *pesebre* by placing the Baby Jesus in his manger.

On December 25, known as *la Navidad*, children often receive presents. However, the traditional day of gift giving is on January 6, the Epiphany or Day of the Three Kings. Because the Three Kings gave gifts to Baby Jesus, children often write letters asking them for gifts. On the eve of the holiday, children fill their shoes with straw as an offering to the Three Kings' camels. Early in the morning, children eagerly run to see if their shoes are full of presents. The Three Kings reward good children with gifts, while bad children receive chunks of coal.

On this holiday, children often get the opportunity to play the *piñata* game. *Piñatas* are clay pots in a variety of shapes, covered with bright crepe paper. The pots are stuffed with candy, peanuts, and other prizes. Children, blindfolded, try to strike the *piñata* with a big stick. Success comes when the *piñata* breaks open and candy spills out. Children merrily scramble to the floor, eagerly gathering up their share of the goodies.

To help celebrate the Day of the Three Kings, Mama bakes a cake called *La Rosca de Reyes* (the King's Ring). A small doll or Christ figurine is hidden in the cake. The person lucky enough to find the doll is treated to a party on February 2, *El Día de la Candelaria* (Candlemas). This party signifies the end of Mexico's six-week holiday season.

NETHERLANDS

GELUKKIG KERSTFEEST

DECORATING THE HOME IS A JOYOUS OCCASION AS
FAMILIES CHOOSE JUST THE RIGHT TREE FROM A LARGE SELECTION
AVAILABLE AT THE CANALS. TREE TRIMMINGS, INCLUDING GLASS
ORNAMENTS, CANDLES, TULIPS, HOLLY, AND MISTLETOE, ARE
PROUDLY DISPLAYED IN NEARBY MARKETS.

Many holiday traditions center around the Netherlands' famous canals and the cold, cloudy winter weather. In fact, an overcast sky lets children and the young at heart know that the Christmas season is on the way.

In mid-November, people gather around the banks of the canals to watch *Sinterklaas* and his sidekick, Black Pete, arrive from Spain in a grand steamer. In some areas, *Sinterklaas*, wearing a bishop's hat, rides his white steed through the streets in extravagant parades. While in town, he also visits children in their schools. Black Pete is never far behind, generously handing out *pepernoten* (spicy cookie balls), chocolate, and oranges from his sack of goodies. Boys and girls are fascinated by Pete because he stuffs naughty children in that very same goody sack and carries them back to Spain for a year of discipline.

On Saint Nicholas Eve, December 5, children set out a pair of wooden shoes for *Sinterklaas* to fill with gifts. Before bed, children leave carrots and hay in the shoes for *Sinterklaas'* horse. As children sleep, *Sinterklaas* rides his steed from one rooftop to another, filling the shoes with gifts. In addition to the goodies left in their shoes, some fortunate children "seek and find" presents hidden in cupboards and drawers throughout the house.

Once Saint Nicholas Day is over, families prepare for Christmas. Decorating the home is a joyous occasion as families choose just the right tree from a large selection available at the canals. Tree trimmings, including glass ornaments, candles, tulips, holly, and mistletoe, are proudly displayed in nearby markets.

The holiday season is a great time to socialize with friends and family. Skating is never more popular than during the Christmas season. Costumed groups gather at frozen canals for skating races. After a cold afternoon, skaters warm up with a piping hot bowl of split pea soup and warm milk flavored with anise. Attending concerts, such as Handel's *Messiah*, is also a popular activity, especially for adults.

Families rise early on Christmas morning and attend church services. The rest of the day is shared with family. Towards evening, the family gathers for Christmas supper. The table is set with a white tablecloth, red and white candles, and a poinsettia centerpiece. The traditional entrée is usually ham, although hare and goose are also popular. Other favorite dishes include savory vegetable soup with fried meatballs and *bessensappudding* (a tart currant pudding).

At the end of an exciting day, children are treated to *marzipan* (almond paste candy shaped as fruits, vegetables, and sausages), homemade *banquet* (dough filled with almond paste, shaped as wreaths, and topped with green and red cherries), and hot chocolate before they are tucked into bed for the night. As the children sleep, adults relax while they slowly enjoy pastries, coffee, and a steaming serving of *bisschopswijn* (a hot spiced wine flavored with cloves and cinnamon).

NORWAY

GOD JUL

CHILDREN ARE AWESTRUCK AT THE SIGHT OF THE COMPLETED
TREE. WHITE CANDLES COMPLEMENT NORWAY'S FLAG, WHICH
SERVES AS GARLAND, AND HANDMADE STRAW ORNAMENTS.

Church bells grandly ring in the holidays late in the afternoon on Christmas Eve. Prior to the ringing bells, everyone scurries around cleaning house, baking good things to eat, and completing last minute chores in preparation for the fourteen-day holiday season.

In the spirit of Christmas, families share their good fortune with birds, animals, and even the family elf. On Christmas Eve, it is customary to hang wheat shocks on poles as an offering to the sparrows. The ground beneath the pole is cleared, giving the birds a place to dance in between feedings. A good year of crops is expected if the father sees a crowd of sparrows eating the wheat. In honor of the animals who witnessed Christ's birth many years ago, extra portions of good things to eat are added to the animals' feeding troughs. Even the little gnome-like figure who protects the family farm is not forgotten. Children leave him a hot bowl of porridge in the barn.

Nothing can interfere with the Christmas Eve festivities, not even the witches who are said to be lurking in and around the homes of Norway. To prohibit the witches from spoiling such a wonderful holiday, all the brooms are hidden after the family's big feast and before opening gifts. Witches have been known to steal the brooms, their means of transportation, when the family is busy opening presents. Crackling spruce logs send sparks up the chimney, preventing the witches from entering the home, and lights are left on throughout the night to scare away evil spirits. Not everyone is banned from the Norwegian home during the holidays. A single candle burns brightly in the window, welcoming travelers, for nobody should be alone on Christmas.

Before the traditional Christmas Eve meal, family members gather at the dinner table and read the family Bible. Before eating the main course of lute-fisk, pork cutlets, or codfish, the family first must eat a bowl of rice porridge. In keeping with Scandinavian tradition, one almond hides in a single bowl of porridge. The person who finds the almond will have good luck next year.

Behind closed doors, parents painstakingly decorate a carefully selected Christmas tree. Children are awestruck at the sight of the completed tree. White candles complement Norway's flag, which serves as garland, and handmade straw ornaments. In honor of the Magi, three candles placed at the very top of the tree illuminate the room. Wrapped presents are stacked underneath, making the sight of the tree all the more appealing. The gifts are brought by *Julebukk* (Christmas buck), an elf who takes on the likeness of a goat. He is a generous soul who leaves gifts and goodies for the children. Before gifts can be opened, hand in hand, the family circles the tree, singing Christmas carols.

Norwegians fill their Christmas Day going to church and reflecting on the meaning of Christmas. The good feelings of the season last through January 6, the feast of the Epiphany. As another holiday season ends, families fondly remember the special moments of the Christmas season.

PHILIPPINES

MALIGAYANG PASKO

FAMILIES USE THEIR INGENUITY TO DECORATE MAKESHIFT
TREES OF BRANCHES, CARDBOARD, OR PALM LEAVES. THE TREES
ARE DECORATED WITH CONICAL HATS, BAMBOO CHAINS, AND
PURCHASED ORNAMENTS POPULAR IN THE WEST.

The Christmas season officially begins on December 16 with nine consecutive early morning Masses called *Misa de Gallo* (Mass of the Rooster). However, signs of Christmas begin appearing in October. Carols are played on the radio and decorations appear in stores and on streets. The Philippine population proudly considers their Christmas season the longest and merriest in the world.

Nothing symbolizes the spirit of the Filipino Christmas better than the *parol*, a paper and bamboo lantern representing the Star of Bethlehem. During the Christmas season, *parols* are placed in windows and on top of Christmas trees. Long ago, the Holy Family sought shelter so that Mary could give birth to her Baby in safety and comfort. Mary and Joseph do not have to look any further than the home in which this lacy paper lantern shines. The *parol* can be purchased in shops around the Islands; however, most families feel that the true meaning of Christmas will be missed if this Star of Bethlehem is not homemade.

Having a live Christmas tree is practically unheard of for all but the wealthiest of families. Because of western influences, the tree has become an increasingly popular decoration. Most families use their ingenuity to decorate makeshift trees of branches, cardboard, or palm leaves. The trees are decorated with conical hats, bamboo chains, and purchased ornaments popular in the west.

On Christmas Eve, after Midnight Mass, a midnight repast called *Noche Buena* is shared among family. *Arroz Caldo* (chicken rice soup with chicken meat), steamed rice cakes, Chinese ham, cheese, bread, and fruit are typically served.

Church bells fill the air on Christmas Day, when all the townspeople are notified that Christmas has arrived. A Christmas Day Mass is offered for those who were unable to attend Midnight Mass. After Mass, children visit their godparents. As a sign of respect, the child places the elder's hand on his or her forehead and whispers *Mano po* (please extend your hand in blessing). After this warm moment, godparents pass out gifts to their godchildren. A Christmas day *fiesta* (party), featuring roasted pig, stuffed chicken, fish, pastries, and casseroles, is shared with family and friends.

It is not uncommon to attend large gatherings on Christmas Day for singing, dancing, and playing games such as *pabitin*. During this game, children try to grab goodies held in a bamboo net. *Palo sebo* is also popular with children (but perhaps not by the person in charge of laundry). For this game, children attempt to climb a greased bamboo pole in order to claim the prize waiting at the top.

The festivities end on January 6 with the Feast of the Epiphany. The longest Christmas season in the world is celebrated with good nature and joy, with the spirit and meaning of Christmas always close to the heart.

POLAND

WESOLYCH SWIAT

CAREFULLY PRESERVED EGGS, SYMBOLIZING REBIRTH, ARE
TRANSFORMED BY LOVING HANDS INTO ORNAMENTS RESEMBLING
DOVES, THE SYMBOL FOR PEACE; ROOSTERS, SYMBOLIZING HEALTH
AND FERTILITY; AND STORKS, WHICH STAND FOR GOOD LUCK.

The Christmas season officially begins on the first day of Advent. For children, however, the holiday season begins on Saint Nicholas Day, December 6. The kind and compassionate Saint Nicholas holds a special place in his heart for orphaned children whom he comforts with small gifts.

Many preparations must be made in order for the holidays to be celebrated properly. Cooks from all over the land begin making *piernik* (a baked honey cake). So special is this delicacy that in generations past, the recipe became part of a woman's dowry.

Women clean their homes to ward off evil spirits that lurk in the dust. Once the home is clean, it can be decorated for the holidays. Christmas ornaments are made by hand at this time. A variety of stars are hand cut in intricate patterns. Carefully preserved eggs, symbolizing rebirth, are transformed by loving hands into ornaments resembling doves, the symbol for peace; roosters, symbolizing health and fertility; and storks, which stand for good luck. Corn kernels, peas, or beans, strung during the harvest, are dried and painted to make bright strings of garland.

On Christmas Eve, everyone must fast all day. Straw is spread out under the table as a reminder that Jesus was born in a stable, while the *crèche* is set up to further remind the family of Christ's birth night. At the table, an extra place is set in anticipation of a visit from a stranger or the Holy Spirit. Small gifts of cookies and coins are placed at each plate. Only after a child sees the first star appear in the sky can family members sit down at the table and break the *oplatek*, a wafer blessed by the priest. One by one, each person takes a wafer and exchanges good wishes, which symbolize the goodwill and peace of the season.

The twelve-course meatless banquet may include herring, carp, or pike; borscht; fruit compote; *pierogis* filled with sauerkraut and mushrooms; and *kutia*.

After the meal, the family enjoys singing *kolendy* (Christmas carols), opening gifts, and decorating the tree. Everyone attends Midnight Mass, where Christmas Day is welcomed by everyone with pleasure.

PUERTO RICO

FELICES PASCUAS

Most of the Christmas decorations appear outside. Nothing is more beautiful at this time than the giant poinsettia bushes that grow in front of homes. The brilliant red plants are in full bloom during the holidays.

Christmas in Puerto Rico centers around family and the Christ Child. The season begins on Christmas Eve, December 24, and ends on January 12, Bethlehem Day. Lighted homes and streets, as well as joyous activity, help make the island brightly festive.

Most of the Christmas decorations appear outside. Nothing is more beautiful at this time than the giant poinsettia bushes that grow in front of homes. The brilliant red plants are in full bloom during the holidays. Considered the Puerto Rican Christmas tree, these bushes grow as tall as six to eight feet. Nativity scenes, featuring life-size wooden figures, appear in some front yards. Intricately carved, they are not damaged by the elements.

Families also decorate artificial pine or fir trees, which are placed outside under the carport. Although some real trees are imported onto the island, the heat prevents real trees from looking fresh. Both types of Christmas trees are decorated with colored lights and topped with a Star of Bethlehem. A nativity scene always appears underneath the Christmas tree. Miniature *cuatros* (small guitars), *maracas* (gourds filled with dried seeds), *guiros* (textured gourd instruments scratched with picks), and *palitos* (little sticks) are common ornaments that serve to honor the *parranda*, a festive and merry holiday tradition.

A *parranda* consists of musicians who travel from house to house making unannounced visits. The musicians perform the songs of the season called *aguinaldos* (gifts). These gifts are sung as an oral tribute to the families living in the homes. It is only right to reward these hardworking musicians with small gifts and a meal in return. A hostess always is prepared for such visits. During this season, she keeps chicken in the freezer so that *asopao* (chicken rice soup) can be prepared in a hurry.

In additional to attending Mass, families enjoy a great Christmas Eve feast. The main course is a whole roasted pig. *Arroz con pollo* (rice and chicken) and *pasteles* are also traditional cuisine. *Pasteles* are very complicated meat pies filled with ground pork and wrapped with a mixture of ground root vegetables such as green bananas and plantains. The *pasteles* are wrapped again with banana leaves and steamed. It is so time-consuming that families enjoy this treat only during the holidays.

For children, the highlight of the holiday season is Three Kings' Day. On this day, the Magi, riding on top of camels, make a great journey from the Orient. In anticipation of their visit, children place boxes filled with grass and bowls of water for the weary camels. During the night, when all are asleep, the camels eat their fill, and the Wise Men leave gifts for the generous children.

The season ends on January 12, Bethlehem Day, when children dress as their favorite nativity characters and parade through the streets for all to see. What a happy time in Puerto Rico!

REPUBLIC OF SLOVAKIA

VASELÉ VIANOCE

CHRISTMAS TREES ARE DECORATED WITH STRAW ORNAMENTS, COOKIES HUNG FROM RIBBON, *salonky*, WALNUTS, APPLES, AND PINE CONES FOUND IN THE FOREST. IN EARLIER TIMES, THE FAMILY HUNG THE CHRISTMAS TREE FROM A CEILING BEAM.

In this eastern European country, Christmas is a time for peace and forgiveness. From December 6, *Svaty Mikuláš* (Saint Nicholas) Day, to January 6, *Tri Kràle* (Three Kings' Day), the family celebrates the joyous Yuletide season with love and reconciliation in mind.

As the season begins, children expect a visit from their old friend *Mikuláš* (Saint Nicholas). Traveling with the Devil and a beautiful, kind angel, *Mikuláš* expects children to place their shoes on the windowsill before his arrival on December 5. As the sun rises, children jump out of bed to look for signs that *Mikuláš* has been to their houses. Good boys and girls find their shoes filled with candies, chocolates, nuts, and fruit, delicacies available only during the holiday season. Bad children receive the humiliating gift of coal. On rare occasions, *Mikuláš* will honor children with a personal visit. In those instances, children must make a solemn vow to be good children all year round. If judged to be sincere, *Mikuláš* will reward them with gifts. What a joy to be rewarded by *Mikuláš*.

The true meaning of Christmas cannot be enjoyed properly until all conflicts, big or small, are resolved. Family members and neighbors take great pains to make peace with each other before the traditional Christmas dinner. In keeping with the theme of respecting others, borrowed items are returned to the proper owners, arguments are settled, ruffled feathers are smoothed, and hurt feelings are mended.

After the family makes peace with others, the floor under the table must be painted with sparkling whitewash. To symbolize family unity and acknowledge family ties, the table legs are chained with thick, strong iron. Today, as it was long ago, Christmas trees are decorated with straw ornaments, cookies hung from ribbon, *salonky* (candies), walnuts, apples, and pine cones found in the forest. In earlier times, the family hung the Christmas tree from a ceiling beam. Although this practice has faded through the years, some families continue this unique tradition.

Before the meal begins, fish scales are placed under each plate to symbolize wealth and abundance. When a child announces that the first star has appeared in the night sky, the family joins in song. To protect her family from evil, the mother makes a cross on everyone's forehead. *Oplátky* (special Christmas Eve wafers) are embossed with Christmas scenes. Fish, symbolizing the Last Supper, golden crusty bread, sauerkraut soup, and potatoes are popular Christmas Eve fare.

After that scrumptious meal, relatives and friends come calling and are rewarded with pastries, bacon, or warm drinks. Before attending Midnight Mass, they gather to sing Christmas carols. Knowing that all is forgiven, people from around the country have the peace of mind and lightness of heart that are indescribably Christmas.

ROMANIA

SARBATORI FERICITE

IN THE OLD ROMANIAN TRADITION, THE FIR TREE REPRESENTS
THE PERMANENCE OF LIFE. IT IS BELIEVED THE CHRISTMAS TREE
ORIGINATED FROM THE THREE MAGI WHO WANTED TO
BESTOW GIFTS UPON THE CHRIST CHILD.

Theater pageants and puppet shows play a large role in the Romanian Christmas celebration. How thrilling for children to reenact Jesus' birth for a willing and appreciative audience! In fact, during the Christmas season, children look forward to the many Christmas rituals which emphasize the importance of this religious holiday. From decorating the Christmas tree to retrieving a cross, the Christmas season is filled with valuable lessons.

In the old Romanian tradition, the fir tree represents the permanence of life. It is believed the Christmas tree originated from the three Magi who wanted to bestow gifts upon the Christ Child. Traditional ornaments, such as red apples, walnuts, cones from the tree, and handcrafted balls, represent the riches given to the Baby Jesus by the Three Kings. A star, which helped guide the Three Wise Men to Baby Jesus, tops the tree and is complemented by handcrafted dolls, which symbolize the purity of all children. Western European-influenced ornaments, such as glass balls, garland, and candles, also grace the tree. Finally, a table containing fasting foods, boiled wheat, bread, and dried fruits, is placed next to the tree. Once complete, the Christmas tree, aglow with white candles and sparkling ornaments, fills the home with a special feeling of warmth.

Christmas Eve is especially fun for boys who travel the neighborhood singing Christmas greetings called *colinde*. The marching through the streets continues on Christmas Day, as the boys gather again to carry a *steaua* (shining star) attached to a long pole. The star's center features a picture of the Holy Family and the Magi. Illuminated from within by a candle, it is decorated with bells, shiny paper, and ribbons. Throughout the streets, the boys sing the beautiful songs of the season with all their might and are amply rewarded with apples, cakes, and coins.

Sarmale (stuffed cabbage) takes center stage at Christmas supper. It is accompanied by *colac* (wheat loaf), turkey in aspic, cheese-stuffed eggs, meatball soup, and a torte filled with chocolate meringue. Another popular dessert is *turte*, dough rolled in layers and filled with walnuts and honey. This doughy mass is shaped into leaves, which represent Baby Jesus' swaddling clothes.

"The Great Blessing of the Waters" is an ancient tradition still enjoyed in Romania today. People in the community gather at the river bank and sing *colinde* (carols). People, dressed in elaborate costumes, act out the parts of Pontius Pilate and Herod. A boy breaks the ice of the river, and the parish priest throws a cross into the water. The people who witness this act scurry into the icy cold water to retrieve the beloved cross. The person who rescues the cross has saved the day and will have good luck all next year. Reaffirming one's faith in the cross is a wonderful way to begin the New Year.

SCOTLAND

NOLLAG CHRIDHEIL

CHILDREN PLAY WITH THE TOYS THEY RECEIVED FROM
SANTA CLAUS AND ENJOY THE GOODIES LEFT FOR THEM IN THEIR
STOCKINGS, WHICH INCLUDE TANGERINES, NOT ALWAYS AVAILABLE IN
DECEMBER; APPLES; AND ONE OR TWO COINS.

Part of the United Kingdom, Scotland lies in the northern part of Great Britain. Christmas is a minor holiday in the Scottish culture and is observed strictly as a religious holiday. In days past, Christmas was not a recognized holiday, and many heads of households had to work on that day. However, the family would attend church services on Christmas morning, as they do today, spending the day quietly at home with family.

Children play with the toys they received from Santa Claus and enjoy the goodies left for them in their stockings, which include tangerines, not always available in December; apples; and one or two coins. Parents give their children small gifts, while Santa provides a large toy like a train set, a doll and buggy, or a truck. Christmas dinner is scheduled either before or after 3:00 p.m. At that time, all activity stops, and the family heads for the television set to watch the Queen's annual Christmas address.

The holiday spirit explodes with joy during the *Hogmanay* (New Year's Eve). This is when the lively fun begins! A national holiday, *Hogmanay*, is Scotland's largest, most-anticipated celebration. The festivities begin early on New Year's Eve and carry on until the wee hours of the morning. The *Hogmanay* takes the form of an "open house," where folks drop in for an evening of frolicking. The host encourages everyone to take part in the festivities by singing, dancing, telling stories, or playing a favorite musical instrument.

A delicious and popular treat, *clootie dumplings* are similar to a fruitcake. Hidden in the *clootie dumplings* are silver coins. When the rich fruitcake is presented to the guests, it quickly disappears as everyone clamors for the coins hidden inside. As tempting as it is to gobble down this delicious treat, great care must be taken to avoid breaking teeth on one of the coins.

Around midnight, all the guests gather around to sing "Auld Lang Syne," a song written by Scottish poet Robert Burns. At midnight, the host opens both the front and back doors to let out the old year and let in the New Year.

Whether a family will have good luck during the New Year depends entirely on the first person to enter the home immediately after the stroke of midnight. In a custom called "first footing," the family will be exceptionally lucky if a tall, dark, and handsome man is the first person to cross over the threshold. The "first foot" usually gives the host a lump of coal and an orange, wishing the family the good fortune to have a warm hearth and food on the table. In turn, the host offers the "first foot" a drink or treat, which he must swallow whole. *Hogmanay* is such a happy time that no can help but have a great start to the New Year!

SERBIA

HRISTOS SE RODI

AS THEY RETURN HOME WITH THREE LOGS FROM THE TREE,
THE MOTHER GREETS THE MEN AND SPRINKLES WHEAT GRAIN
OVER THE FATHER'S HEAD FOR GOOD LUCK.

Located in the western Balkans, Serbia, in accordance with the Julian calendar, celebrates Christmas on January 7. Forty days before Christmas, people begin fasting to cleanse their bodies and souls for the birth of Jesus.

The holiday season begins with St. Nicholas Day. On the eve of this feast, December 19, children take great pains to polish their shoes for St. Nicholas, who will visit in the night to fill them with gifts, nuts, and fruit. Wheat grains, soaked in water, are planted in a dish and faithfully tended until Christmas Day. It is believed that the family will have a good harvest if the wheat grows thick and lush.

On the morning of Christmas Eve, the males of the household go out in search of a *Badnjak* (Yule log). When the father selects a perfect oak tree, a prayer is offered and the tree is cut down. As they return home with three logs from the tree, the mother greets the men and sprinkles wheat grain over the father's head for good luck. The *Badnjak* is put on the fireplace, and the father blesses the log with wheat, wine, and oil, while praying for health and success in the New Year. Once this initial offering is made, each guest entering the home also must sprinkle wheat onto the *Badnjak*, expressing good wishes to the family, while the sparks fly.

Once the *Badnjak* catches fire, the father leaves the room, returning as *Božić Bata*, or "Brother Christmas." He is loaded down with straw and begins clucking like a chicken. The mother joins him, while the children follow, cheeping like baby chicks. Together, they spread straw over the floors to resemble the humble stable where Baby Jesus was born. The host takes great handfuls of walnuts and throws them into the corners of the room, symbolizing the sign of the cross.

Once the home is prepared, the family sits down for a meal that is still within the keeping of the fast. The family enjoys codfish, vegetables, dried fruit, and nuts. As the clock strikes twelve, the family leaves to attend Christmas Eve worship services.

On Christmas Day, everyone eagerly waits for the first male guest to enter the home. He is sprinkled with wheat, kissed on each cheek, and served a small glass of hot plum brandy. In turn, he throws out a handful of coins for the children to gather up. This honored guest is expected to stay throughout the day's celebration.

A great feast, featuring a suckling pig and cabbage rolls, officially breaks the fast. The *božičnjak* (ornately decorated Christmas sweet bread) is placed lovingly on the table but is not eaten until the New Year. Instead, the family eats a *česnica*, another Christmas bread, which is passed around as everyone pulls apart his/her own piece. Baked in the bread is a gold or silver coin. The person lucky enough to find the coin in his/her slice of bread will have a lucky piece to carry with him/her during the New Year.

SLOVENIA

VESELE BOZICNE PRAZNKE

CHILDREN DELIGHT IN ACCOMPANYING PARENTS INTO THE FOREST
TO COLLECT THE BEST BITS OF MOSS AND THE SMALLEST PINE
SEEDLINGS FOR THE CRÈCHE'S NATURAL-LOOKING BACKGROUND. THE
WOODEN FIGURINES ARE PLACED ON A NEW, WHITE, HAND-STITCHED
DOILY, MADE ESPECIALLY FOR THIS OCCASION.

The month-long Yuletide season begins on Saint Nicholas Day, December 6, and ends one month later with the Festival of the Three Kings. In this northwesternmost part of the former Yugoslavia, Christmas centers around God, Christ, and prayer. Children and adults celebrate the birth of Baby Jesus by seeking out and enjoying the simple pleasures of the season.

Children can hardly wait for Saint Nicholas to arrive in town! Dressed in a flowing white robe trimmed in gold, Saint Nicholas wears a tall white bishop's hat on his head. He travels with the "devils" and an angel who never leave his side. Naughty children often are worried they will get a sound scolding from the devils, for bad behavior. However, they know that the angel will bring presents to all children who have goodness in their hearts.

As part of the Christmas preparations, the entire family takes pleasure in setting up "God's corner," the main home decoration. Designed to hold the family's crèche, the father gets the honor of setting the pyramid-shaped shelving unit in a corner of the main room of the home. It is quite a family event preparing "God's corner." Children delight in accompanying parents into the forest to collect the best bits of moss and the smallest pine seedlings for the crèche's natural-looking background. The wooden figurines are placed on a new, white, hand-stitched doily, made especially for this occasion. On Christmas Eve, all members of the family circle around "God's corner" and pray. With holy water, the family blesses each room of the home, as well as the barns, sheds, stables, and fields.

On Christmas Eve night, families walk to church in unity. They carry torches to light their way to church while singing the festive songs of the Yuletide season. After Mass, the family breaks a one-day fast, enjoying a small ham, *potica* (sweet bread with walnuts), and a variety of home-baked cookies. *Poprtnjak* (bread that is covered with cloth) is prepared specially for this meal and set on the table. The family is allowed a taste of this good bread on the three holiest nights: Christmas Eve, New Year's Eve, and the Three Kings Eve.

The Festival of the Three Kings marks the end of the holiday season. Children travel from house to house carrying lighted star-shaped lanterns, their young voices rejoicing in song. Celebrating the simplicity of the season brings out the true meaning of Christmas.

SWEDEN

GOD JUL

IN MANY HOMES, A SPECIAL LITTLE TREE FILLED WITH
COOKIES AND CANDY IS GIVEN AS A GIFT TO SMALL CHILDREN. THE
BOYS AND GIRLS HAPPILY POUNCE ON THAT TREE AND MAKE
THE COOKIES DISAPPEAR QUICKLY.

Families all over Sweden look forward to lighting the Advent candles, the symbolic beginning to the festive Christmas season. Before the big day, the family has much to do. To make the work go by quickly, the family cleans the house together to make it sparkling and fresh for Christmas. Spicy smells fill the kitchen as gingerbread men bake in the oven. To encourage light to return to the land, many candles are lit and placed in the home and church.

The day before Christmas Eve, the family sets out to find a Christmas tree in the forest. With keen eyes, parents look for a lush and shapely tree. Children assist them by looking for a bird's nest, which might be tucked in between the branches. Finding such a nest ensures the family good luck. Once the perfect tree is selected, it is placed in the middle of the living room and decorated with heart-shaped baskets made from woven straw. These baskets are stuffed with candy, which will be gobbled up on January 13, Saint Knut's Day. Handmade straw ornaments shaped like animals, the Swedish flag, and *Julgrans Karameller* (candy-filled cardboard rings covered with tissue paper) also are added to the tree.

It is said that a little gnome named Tomte lives under the floorboards of each home or barn in Sweden. All year long, Tomte keeps busy, ensuring the safety of the family and the livestock. On Christmas Eve, he comes out of the floor, carrying a sack of gifts, which he personally gives to the children.

During the traditional Christmas Eve smorgasbord, it is great fun to take part in the "dipping in the pot." Before the meal begins, family members dip slices of homemade bread into the ham drippings. As they enjoy the fresh bread dipped in the tangy, caramelized ham juice, the family honors their ancestors who may not have been so fortunate. In addition to the ham, the table is full of luscious things to eat, like *lutfisk* (a white fish soaked in lye) drowned in melted butter, jellied pigs' feet, rice porridge, sausages, meatballs, herring, salad, cakes, and cookies. Nobody goes hungry during this meal.

On Christmas morning, the family rises early to attend church and spends Christmas afternoon visiting friends and family and eating homemade treats. In earlier times before cars, families would go to church in sleighs. Neighboring families would race to see who could get to church first. This good-natured race was great fun, and the winning family would receive good luck.

The joyous Christmas season ends on Saint Knut's Day. On this day, children are allowed to eat the treats left on the Christmas tree. In many homes, a special little tree filled with cookies and candy is given as a gift to small children. The boys and girls happily pounce on that tree and make the cookies disappear quickly. When it is dark across the land, all the Christmas trees are taken down. Towns sponsor bonfires, and families throw their trees on a great pile of fire. People gather to watch the great flames as the trees burn to smoldering embers.

SWITZERLAND

FROEHLICHE WEINACHTEN

JOYEUX NOËL

BUON NATALE

NADEL

THE TREE MUST BE DECORATED IN STRICT SECRECY.
PARENTS WILL CHASE THEIR CHILDREN OUT OF THE HOUSE,
A TRADITION MOST FAMILIES LOOK FORWARD TO WITH GLEE.

Switzerland's holiday traditions are a swirling together of the French, German, Austrian, and Italian cultures. Over the centuries, landlocked Switzerland has adopted many traditions of the countries that share its borders. With the majestic Alps and Jura Mountains in the background, Switzerland is truly a sight to behold during this international Yuletide season.

Throughout the holidays, Switzerland's many regions host a number of gift-giving spirits. On December 5, in Kussnacht, hundreds of people join in a parade during the "Pursuit of Saint Nicholas." Leading the parade, whip crackers joyfully sound the arrival of Saint Nicholas. Following behind are strong men, ringing heavy metal bells. A brass band with blowing horns makes merry music along the streets. More than two hundred people, proudly wearing lace-patterned bishops' hats (well over six feet tall), bring up the rear of this noisy and spirited procession.

On December 6, the people of Fribourg watch Saint Nicholas arrive in their city, riding his faithful donkey. At the town square, members of the community gather together for a delectable banquet and listen to a speech given by none other than Saint Nicholas himself. A tiny angel, *Christkindli*, arrives at each house with the tinkling of silver bells. She glides through each home in a white gown and veil, her head topped by a jewel-covered crown. She and her little child helpers give presents from her basket. In other regions, *Samichlaus* (Father Christmas) and his wife *La Befana* (Lucy) all treat children to candy and presents during the happiest time of the year.

The house is not ready for Christmas until the tree is brought in the home and decorated. Since the tree must be decorated in strict secrecy, parents must chase their children out of the house, a tradition most children look forward to with glee. In peace and quiet, the parents carefully decorate the tree with clear glass bulbs, candles, cookies, and candy.

On Christmas Eve, many families wait impatiently for their grandmothers to predict the future. With many years of experience, grandmother carefully fills twelve separate onion layers with salt. On Christmas morning, she is able to predict the weather by the salt's condition: dry salt means people can enjoy mild weather, while wet salt means a rainy season lies ahead.

Bell ringing is very much part of Switzerland's Christmas celebration. Churches from neighboring villages compete with each other to announce that Midnight Mass is about to begin. Upon hearing these rich, clear tones in the cold night air, families set out for church. After Mass is over, the Christmas celebration continues as families indulge in *marzipan* (almond paste candy), Tirggel cookies, and *ringli* (homemade doughnuts), stretching the merriment of Christmas far into the night.

UKRAINE

VESELYKH SVYAT

To get eager children to sleep, parents tell the story about Father Frost and the little Snowflake Girl and how dreams of the good can come true.

Ukrainian holiday traditions are influenced largely by Lithuanian and Polish cultures. The season begins on Christmas Eve, January 6. For three days, family and friends gather to sing, dance, and enjoy the delicious holiday foods among good company.

To prepare for Christmas, every room in the house is cleaned from top to bottom. It is considered good luck to find a spider in the house during the holidays. This belief dates back to an old folk tale. On the dirt floor in a small hut where an old widow lived with her small children, a pine tree began to grow where a squirrel had dropped a nut. The widow and her children cared for the tree, hoping it would grow big and strong. On Christmas Eve, the widow was saddened because she could not provide decorations for the tree. During the night, spiders spun delicate webs on the tree, and when the first rays of light touched the tree, the webs magically turned to silver. The grateful widow never wanted for anything again, and trees in the Ukraine are decorated with silver spider webs.

A beautiful table is set for the twelve-course, meatless meal. Straw is placed on the table, which is covered with an embroidered tablecloth. A large *kolach* (braided bread) serves as the centerpiece. A candle and a bowl of *kutia* (wheat mixed with honey and poppy seeds) are placed in the window to honor the souls of the family's ancestors. An extra place is set at the table for a stranger.

Once the first star appears in the sky, the family savors delicious *borsch* (beet soup), *vushky* (dumplings) with mushroom filling, baked fish with aspic, *halibuts* (stuffed cabbage rolls), *uzvar* (fruit compote), and *pampushky* (doughnuts). An enjoyable, yet sticky, tradition calls for the head of the household to throw the first spoonful of *kutia* on the ceiling. The more *kutia* that sticks to the ceiling, the more luck the family will have for the New Year. After everyone finishes eating, the family members sing their favorite carols until they leave shortly before midnight to attend the Nativity Divine Liturgy.

Children look forward to a visit from Father Frost and the little Snowflake Girl. Father Frost travels by sleigh pulled by three reindeer. To get eager children to sleep, parents tell the story about the snow child and how dreams of the good can come true. A lonely old couple longed for a child to love. The old woman carefully stitched a pair of tiny white slippers for the child of her dreams. The next morning, a tiny snow child magically appeared. The snow child danced about the ground and windows, leaving a sparkling bright layer of beautiful white snow. The snow child was very happy living outside in the cold, glorious snow. She never went inside the house because she could not stand the warmth. In the spring, the snow child would leave the old couple, which made them very sad. But every winter, she would come home to her beloved parents and create beauty for them to enjoy.

WALES

NADOLIG LLAWEN

Handcrafted ornaments that adorn the Christmas tree reflect the customs and spirit of Wales. Mistletoe and holly are tucked into the branches of the Christmas tree.

Singing to the heart's content marks the Welsh Christmas. During the season in this southeastern area of the United Kingdom, children and adults alike gather from all over the country to attend and participate in choir contests. This musical holiday season begins on Christmas Day, December 25, and ends on the Feast of Epiphany, January 6. Some families make the merriment last until Candlemas on February 2.

Homes are decorated with mistletoe and holly, plants said to hold magical powers. Handcrafted ornaments that adorn the Christmas tree reflect the customs and spirit of Wales. Mistletoe and holly are tucked into the branches of the Christmas tree. *Calennig* (apple ornaments), wrens, and hand-carved *Mari Lwyd* (hobbyhorses decorated in ribbons of festive colors), all represent traditions and ceremonies that shape the Welsh Christmas season.

Love spoons, which date back before the seventeenth century, also bring beauty and significance to the Christmas tree. The Welsh love spoon, in particular, is a unique tradition. A young man would carve a spoon for the woman he wanted to marry. A kind of engagement ring, the more intricately carved the spoon, the more value was placed on it. The spoon's uniqueness was limited only by the carver's skill and imagination. A spoon with a heart meant "my heart is yours," a wheel or spade meant that the man would work hard for his wife. If the woman accepted the man's proposal, she would hang the spoon above the kitchen door in their new home. Many families hang love spoons on their trees to honor this tradition passed down through the generations.

In the wee hours of Christmas morning, families attend *plygain*, a church service in which the community sings Christmas carol after carol. These carols are highly regarded. Poets and families alike strive to come up with the best lyrics representing Welsh customs and lifestyles.

Once the *plygain* is over, the rest of Christmas Day is spent at home. The family enjoys a meal featuring roasted goose, and during the evening, the whole family participates in a taffy pull.

New Year's Day and the Twelfth Night provide enjoyable customs, all of which include singing. On New Year's Day, children visit their neighbors for the *calennig* (the giving of gifts). Carrying decorated apples, the children sing songs about the New Year. They are rewarded with money, treats, or food. During Hunting the Wren, people place a wren in a ribboned bird house. The wren is carried in a procession, while people sing songs in celebration. On January 5, the Twelfth Night, a leader holding a decorated horse's skull travels through the streets during the *Mari Lwyd*. The skull is attached to a long pole and is draped with a white cloth. The horses' jaw is rigged with a spring that makes an impressive snapping noise. If the horse bites a villager, that person must pay a fine.

At the end of the glorious holiday season, families look forward to a whole new year of singing the carols of the season.

Bai-nien

Once the home is sparkling, the family will decorate the home with flowers and place a money tree, made from cypress or pine branches, in an area of prominence. Children have fun hanging coins, paper flowers, and other adornments from its branches.

Good wishes and gratitude for a safe and happy year are passed along to all on the Chinese New Year. The New Year's celebration lasts for nine days, beginning on the first day of the new moon between January 21 and February 20. During that time, there is much to see and do as the country's excitement rises in anticipation of this favorite and most important holiday.

Preparation for the exciting holiday takes many days. The home is cleaned thoroughly, and all work instruments, such as knives, scissors, and brooms, are hidden away. It is believed to be bad luck to use them on New Year's Day. Once the home is sparkling, the family will decorate the home with flowers and place a money tree, made from cypress or pine branches, in an area of prominence. Children have fun hanging coins, paper flowers, and other adornments from its branches. The kitchen is the busiest room in the house. Since cooking is banned on New Year's Day, plenty of food is prepared ahead of time to feed all of the people expected to visit.

With cheerful greetings, the guests arrive for the traditional New Year's Eve feast. The table is a sight to be seen. It is covered with a red cloth (red is China's good luck color) and topped with countless dishes of delectable food, including family members' individual favorites. Gathering around the table, the family lights red candles and makes an offering to the gods. At midnight, it is great fun to seal all of the doors with good luck paper. When the New Year arrives, greetings of "*Bai-nien*" (Happy New Year!) are heard throughout the house and across the country.

In celebration of the New Year, everyone dresses in his/her finest clothes and is treated to a new pair of shoes. Friends exchange red greeting cards, and children are given tangerines, oranges, and small red envelopes filled with coins. To bring good luck to the New Year, families eat special vegetables during a traditional luncheon. For the next several days, children are heard singing in the streets, joyfully welcoming the New Year.

The celebration comes to an end on the day of the first full moon, commemorated with the Feast of Lanterns. The Great Dragon, the Chinese symbol of strength and goodness, leads a parade during the great Feast of Lanterns. People carrying lanterns follow along in this huge parade. In some processions, the Golden Dragon can be quite elaborate, stretching as long as one hundred feet! Men and boys, lucky enough to be granted the honor of carrying the Golden Dragon, skillfully make the great beast seem alive with strength and power.

Legend dictates that the Golden Dragon has been deep asleep for a year. He will remain awake only during the parade and will go back into hibernation when it ends. To prevent the Golden Dragon from falling asleep, people throw firecrackers to block his path. The loudness of the firecrackers ensures he stays awake, keeping the grand celebration and the happy spirit of the day alive.

DIWALI

Deepavali

Diwali IS IDENTIFIED WITH THOUSANDS UPON THOUSANDS
OF *dipas* THAT GLOW AND GLEAM ON THE ROOFTOPS,
BALCONIES, AND WINDOWS OF HOMES AND BUSINESSES
THROUGHOUT THE COUNTRY.

The *Diwali* festival is a very happy time for the people of India. Celebrated in late October or early November, *Diwali's* five-day festival ends on the fifteen day of *Ashwin* (a month according to the Hindu calendar). *Diwali* is identified with thousands upon thousands of *dipas* (oil-burning lamps made from clay, filled with mustard oil, and lit with a hand-rolled cotton wick) that glow and gleam on the rooftops, balconies, and windows of homes and businesses throughout the country. The thought of *Diwali* brings instant joy and anticipation from the very young to the very old. The festival is actually a series of individual holidays that are unrelated except that they are celebrated within the same time span, one right after the other.

Preparation for the *Diwali* festival is time-consuming. The homes are cleaned thoroughly, great amounts of baking are done to make the necessary sweets, and families shop for new outfits to wear during this merry time. One of the most time-consuming preparations is decorating the floors with *alpanas*, intricate designs that look very similar to Indian rugs. *Alpanas* is an ancient technique, requiring great skill. Women take handfuls of rice powder and carefully sift thin streams through their fingers to make intricate patterns on the floor. Once the outline is complete, the women may continue by filling in the outlines with a variety of colored flour. The results are breathtaking yet, sadly, temporary.

Diwali is a time of cleanliness. Some people bathe in perfumed oils, while others bathe in rivers or streams to rid themselves of any evil spirits. Visits to the temple also are necessary to complete the cleansing process.

During one *Diwali* holiday, families share special foods, including a dinner featuring fourteen different dishes to honor the moon, which is said to change its face every fourteen days.

Another *Diwali* celebration honors the legend of Rama. Long ago, Rama was the firstborn son of a beloved king. Legend states that as the king and the queen, his second wife, were traveling, the queen saved the king from a violent death. Grateful for her act of bravery, the king granted the queen a wish, which she saved for another day. That day came when the queen announced that her son, not Rama, would be the successor of the throne. An honorable man, the king had to keep his word. To ensure her own son's success as king, she banished Rama from India for fourteen years. Eventually, when Rama tried to return home, he was lost at sea surrounded by the darkness of the night. The people of India lit thousands of *dipas* to light his way home. Thanks to the love of his devoted followers, and the glowing *dipas*, he safely returned home and took his rightful place as king.

This legend, among others, is what makes the *dipas* so enduring. During *Diwali*, as people survey the land, they admire its beauty and respect the enduring light of the *dipas*.

HANUKKAH

HAPPY HANUKKAH

DURING THE EIGHT DAYS OF *Hanukkah* (DEDICATION),
CANDLES ARE LIT ON AN EIGHT-BRANCHED CANDLESTICK,
CALLED A *menorah*, TO COMMEMORATE THE LEGENDARY MIRACLE
OF LIGHT THAT OCCURRED IN 165 B.C.E.

Hanukkah is a joyous holiday celebrated with songs, psalms, and feasts by Jewish people throughout the world. The Festival of Lights usually begins in late December, on the 25th day of the Jewish month of *Kislev*.

During the eight days of *Hanukkah* (dedication), candles are lit on an eight-branched candlestick, called a *menorah*, to commemorate the legendary miracle of light that occurred in 165 B.C.E. More than two thousand years ago, Antiochus, an unmerciful and vicious Syrian-Greek king, ruled Palestine, the Jewish homeland. Antiochus outlawed the Jewish faith and killed those Jews who dared to practice their religious beliefs.

Mattathias and his five sons would not obey this unreasonable demand and fled to the mountains to prevent their certain deaths. As word got out, an army grew as other faithful Jews followed Mattathias. The army was headed by Judah, Mattathias' son. He acted with such bravery and strength that the army nicknamed him *Maccabee* (meaning Hammer). For many years, the *Maccabees* fought Antiochus and his soldiers until, at last, the Jews were able to reclaim their temple, which was transformed to a place to worship Greek gods. Finally free to worship as they pleased, the *Maccabees* cleaned the temple to make it holy again, but needed oil to burn to dedicate the temple. They had only enough oil to last one night. A miracle occurred when the light lasted for eight days. Because of this miracle, Jewish people celebrate with eight days of Hanukkah.

During this holiday, families gather together each evening to light a candle on the *menorah*, one each night. Children enjoy eating Hanukkah *gelt* (chocolate coins) and playing with the *dreidel* (a square top with Hebrew letters on each side, which together mean "A great miracle happened here"). The family listens to music and visits with friends. Family members exchange gifts. Children often receive one gift each day of the celebration, something they look forward to with great anticipation. Special foods are enjoyed throughout the holiday, particularly ones cooked in oil, such as jelly doughnuts and *potato latkes* (pancakes).

On the last day, all candles on the *menorah* glow, and Jews look upon it as a great symbol of truth and light.

KWANZAA

KWANZAA

FAMILIES OPEN THEIR DOORS DURING THIS CELEBRATION SO THAT *Kwanzaa* CAN BE ENJOYED IN UNITY WITH EXTENDED FAMILY, FRIENDS, AND NEIGHBORS. GUESTS ARRIVE AT THE OPEN HOUSE WEARING THE BRIGHT PRINTS OF TRADITIONAL AFRICAN CLOTHING.

Kwanzaa, which in Swahili means "first fruits of the harvest," is an African American cultural holiday based on seven important principles. The purpose of this holiday is to reaffirm and strengthen the bonds between African Americans. Created by Dr. Maulana Karenga back in 1966, Kwanzaa was influenced by African harvest celebrations, called "the first fruits," and reflects the needs and experiences of African Americans. This seven-day celebration begins on December 26 and lasts until January 1. It is a time for families and friends to spend together, focusing on one's role in life.

On the first evening of *Kwanzaa*, family members gather together around a *kinara* (a seven-tiered candelabra), lighting the candle that corresponds with *umoja* (unity), the first of the seven principles. As the family shares in this moment, the candle burns brightly, and each family member takes a turn discussing what the principle means. Each following night, the family comes together to light additional candles, one for each of the principles of *Kwanzaa*: *kujichagulia* (self-determination), *ujima* (collective work and responsibility), *ujamaa* (cooperative economics), *nia* (purpose), *kuumba* (creativity), and *imani* (faith).

In many homes, families display the seven basic symbols of the *Kwanzaa* celebration. *Mkeka* (mat) symbolizes African history and tradition. It is the foundation on which all other items, including the *kinara*, are placed. Other items include *vibunzi* (ears of corn); *mazao* (crops), representing fresh fruits and vegetables; *mishumaa saba* (seven candles); *kikomba cha umoja* (unity cup); and *zawadi* (gifts).

Kwanzaa is celebrated with a great sense of pride among family and friends. It is customary for host families to open their doors during this celebration so that *Kwanzaa* can be enjoyed in unity with extended family, friends, and neighbors. Guests arrive at the open house wearing the bright prints of traditional African clothing. Throughout the evening, everyone enjoys the occasion by singing, dancing, eating, telling stories, and playing games, all centered around the seven principles. One enjoyable and rewarding game is to place slips of paper into a bowl, listing the names of the seven principles in both English and Swahili. The person who draws *nia* will pair up with the person who draws purpose. During the evening, the pair spends time with each other discussing what this principle means to them, a discussion that is often enlightening, rewarding, and thought-provoking. The seven principles and family togetherness bring out a great sense of pride and community, making *Kwanzaa* a truly special celebration.

SAINT LUCIA DAY

SAINT LUCIA DAY

SAINT LUCIA DAY IS CELEBRATED NOT JUST AT HOME; IT ALSO
IS CELEBRATED AS A COMMUNITY. TEACHERS, POLICEMEN, AND
OTHER PUBLIC SERVANTS ARE HONORED BY LUCIAS WHO SEEK
OUT VALUED MEMBERS OF THE NEIGHBORHOOD.

Early in the morning on December 13, when the rest of the house is fast asleep, the oldest daughter in every Swedish home is in the kitchen preparing good things to eat. Fragrant, hot coffee is brewing, while cookies and raisin-topped *Lucia cats* (saffron buns) bake in the oven. She carefully prepares a tray to serve her parents and siblings breakfast in bed. This is an awesome responsibility shared by all the oldest girls throughout the country, bestowed with the honor of being Saint Lucia, "Queen of Light."

Lucia was a Sicilian girl who lived around 283 A.D. The Romans forbade the worship of Christ, and Lucia was a Christian. It is said that Lucia wanted to serve God and refused a marriage proposal to a man she did not love. In an act of vengeance, her intended husband turned Lucia in to the authorities for her Christian beliefs. The Romans tried to burn her at the stake, but miraculously, the flames did not burn her, and she was not harmed. The Romans finally ended her life with a sword. Because she could not be killed by fire, she was sainted and is now known as the Saint Lucia, "Queen of Light."

On December 13, historically the longest night of the year (according to the old Julian calendar), the people of Sweden look forward to longer days and an end to dark, dreary, and cold weather. A Lucia maiden wears a long, snow-white gown and a red sash tied around her waist. An evergreen wreath sits on her head, upon which lighted candles softly glow. Ever so carefully, she carries the heavy tray to her parents while singing Saint Lucia Day songs. Proudly, she serves her sleeping parents breakfast in bed. Once her parents are served, she graciously brings her tray to each of her brothers and sisters so they too get their fill of delicious saffron buns, fresh from the oven.

Saint Lucia Day is celebrated not just at home; it also is celebrated as a community. Teachers, policemen, and other public servants are honored by Lucias who seek out valued members of the neighborhood, serving them coffee from thermoses and *Lucia cats*. Contests are held to elect "Lucia Brides," who are then featured in parades honoring Saint Lucia. The most famous parade is in Stockholm, Sweden's capital. School children dress in costumes depicting Biblical characters, while "Star Boys," Lucia's attendants, also march along the streets. Pretty girls elected Saint Lucia in area contests wave to the crowd in parade cars or floats. The Lucia who wins the contest in Stockholm is awarded her crown at the end of the parade by that year's recipient of the Nobel Peace Prize for literature.

Depicting Saint Lucia, at home or in Stockholm, is truly an honor that young ladies will hold dear throughout their lives.

SHOGATSU

SHINNEN OMEDETO

NEW YEAR'S DAY IS ESPECIALLY FUN FOR CHILDREN. THROUGHOUT
THE DAY, THEY SPIN TOPS, FLY KITES, AND PLAY BADMINTON WITH
FEATHERED BIRDIES AND BEAUTIFULLY HAND-PAINTED PADDLES.

Shogatsu (Japanese New Year), celebrated on January 1, is the most elaborate holiday of the year. Because families must welcome into their homes their ancestral spirits and the protective *toshigami* (god of the incoming year), the whole family must unite in order to complete preparations for this festive occasion.

Prior to January 1, the house is scrubbed thoroughly for the New Year's feast. At this time, every corner of the home is cleaned, and unneeded clutter is disposed of to make the home organized and pleasing to the eye. Once the home is spotless, each member of the family sips *saké*, takes part in a ritual soaking bath, and savors rich and steaming *okotojiru* (soup made of taro, radish, carrots, and red beans) in order to cleanse body and soul.

On December 13, family members strive to fulfill any personal obligations. The head of the household builds a *kadomatsu*, a decorative display in which the *toshigami* will live. It is at the *kadomatsu* where good health and bounty will flow. The *kadomatsu* is usually made from bamboo or pine branches. It can be of simple or elaborate design.

On New Year's Day, no manual labor or housework is done. Everyone is in high spirits, and children are told to be good because it is believed that how one spends New Year's Day is how one will spend the remainder of the year.

On New Year's morning, the traditional breakfast of savory *ozoni* (hand-pounded, sticky rice cake, *mochi*, in a vegetable soup) is eaten with great relish. People do not dare go the day without eating *ozoni* because to do otherwise would be very unlucky. As the family enjoys this delicious and steaming soup, they wish each other good health and prosperity.

Families and friends spend the day eating dozens of scrumptious dishes, such as *sushi* (rice flavored with rice-vinegar and wrapped in seaweed), meat, fish, seafood, and vegetable dishes. The dinner table is a grand sight to behold, for in the center of the table stands a large centerpiece made from giant, bright red lobsters, which symbolize old age and longevity.

New Year's Day is especially fun for children. Throughout the day, they spin tops, fly kites, and play badminton with feathered birdies and beautifully hand-painted paddles. This game, in particular, is fun for both the winners and the losers. The victor gets to paint the face of the loser, who doesn't really mind gaining attention from the scary or whimsical-looking makeup. It's a joy for one and all.

To order additional copies of

TRADITIONS
or
A SEASON OF CELEBRATING

Mail your order to:
The Museum Shops
Museum of Science and Industry
57th Street and Lake Shore Drive
Chicago, Illinois 60637
or
fax your order to:
(773) 684-8853
or phone:
(773) 684-9844, Ext. 2476
or visit our website: http://www.msichicago.org

When ordering, please provide the following information:
Name, Museum Member Number (for 10% discount), Address,
Zip Code, and Telephone Number

Indicate the Method of Payment:
(Visa, MC, Discover, Amex, Diner or Check or Money Order)

If ordering by mail or fax and paying by credit card indicate:
Credit Card Number, Expiration Date, and Signature

The cost per book is:
Traditions: $19.95
A Season of Celebrating: $15.95
less 10% Museum Member Discount if applicable
(Illinois residents please add 8.75% sales tax)
and include appropriate Shipping and Handling amount
according to the chart below:

Shipping and Handling:

$10.01 to $25.00	$4.50
$25.01 to $40.00	$6.50
$40.01 to $55.00	$7.95
$55.01 to $75.00	$8.50
$75.01 to $100.00	$9.95
$100.00 +	$11.50